Dearest Pratik

Happy

TOI BLOGGERS' PARK

Best wishes always.

Sona

TOI Bloggers' Park

First edition 2011

Published by
Bennett, Coleman & Co. Ltd.,
7, Bahadur Shah Zafar Marg,
New Delhi - 110002

Edited, Designed, Marketed & Distributed by

Times Group Books
(A division of Bennett, Coleman and Company Limited)
Times Annexe, 9-10, Bahadur Shah Zafar Marg, New Delhi-110002

Printed at: Saurabh Printers Pvt. Ltd.

ISBN 978-93-80942-58-2

Price: ₹199

Send your feedback at: editor.tgb@timesgroup.com

Contents

Preface 7

India 9

9 **Why assassinations don't work** —*Pritish Nandy*

12 **As public anger increases, corruption falls** —*SA Aiyar*

15 **Women must seek poribartan now** —*Shobhaa De*

18 **The Pillitzer Prize** —*Bachi Karkaria*

20 **India's racing ahead, but are we on track?** —*TK Arun*

22 **How Binayak Sen became a cause celebre** —*Swapan Dasgupta*

25 **Games a metaphor for all that's wrong with Indian democracy** —*CP Surendran*

28 **The attack of dirty-tricks department** —*Rajesh Kalra*

31 **Lokpal not enough, we need radical reform** —*SA Aiyar*

34 **Mahatma a 'gay' icon? Why not?** —*Shobhaa De*

37 **Khadi or Teflon? Your choice** —*Pritish Nandy*

40 **Kaun Banega Corruptpati?** —*Bachi Karkaria*

42 **War is like an ageing actress** —*Robin David*

45 **The triumph in the tragedy of Aruna Shanbaug** —*Jug Suraiya*

48 **There's a Pakistan beyond the ISI and terror; wish it was stronger** —*Anshul Chaturvedi*

51 **Reforming political funding** —*TK Arun*

54 **Those who allowed pilots with fake licences should be tried for attempt to murder** —*Rajesh Kalra*

56 **How to prevent licensing scams** —*SA Aiyar*

59 **India's shameful load of shit** —*Jug Suraiya*

61 **Sai Baba's one real miracle that no one can question** —*Rajesh Kalra*

63 **Calling Bengali/Bihari V Kuriens** —*TK Arun*

66 **Turn Adarsh into a monument of shame** —*Shobhaa De*

69 **A sense of déjà vu** —*Pritish Nandy*

72 **Is it time to acknowledge the Gujarat 'miracle'?** —*Swapan Dasgupta*

75 **What makes Kashmiri youth angry** —*Rajesh Kalra*

78 **Tackling Maoism: lessons from Andhra** —*SA Aiyar*

81 **No cricket diplomacy, please** —*Robin David*

83 **What PM should learn from Dhoni** —*Shobhaa De*

86 **An encounter with Niira Radia** —*Kingshuk Nag*

89 **Vivekananda: My teen icon wore saffron** —*Anshul Chaturvedi*

92 **A nation of banias** —*Pritish Nandy*

95 **India Inc should look beyond BTech and MBA** —*Swapan Dasgupta*

98 **Cane and able: what a terrible idea, Sirji!** —*Shobhaa De*

101 **Book-banning belongs to a bygone era** —*Robin David*

103 **Act against community crime** —*Nandita Sengupta*

106 **Jugaad is our most precious resource** —*SA Aiyar*

Politics 109

109 **Please don't be silent, Prime Minister** —*Gurcharan Das*

112 **Is the government giving licences to loot the public?** —*Shobhan Saxena*

115 **Support Anna, and all's changed: How naïve are we?** *—Anshul Chaturvedi*

119 **The Teflon Mr Pawar** *—Nauzer K Bharucha*

121 **Is it criminal to think small in India?** *—Gurcharan Das*

124 **What made Niira Radia so powerful** *—Kingshuk Nag*

127 **A tribute to whistle-blowers** *—Nauzer K Bharucha*

129 **Let 'butter' sense prevail** *—Vinita Dawra Nangia*

132 **Good omens for rule of law in India** *—Gurcharan Das*

135 **India must apologise to the Karmapa Lama** *—Shobhan Saxena*

World 139

139 **Osama's death may end bloom of Arab Spring** *—SA Aiyar*

142 **Jihad lives on after bin Laden** *—TK Arun*

144 **Questions for Pakistan** *—Indrani Bagchi*

147 **The most powerful man in the world** *—CP Surendran*

149 **Tragic triumph** *—Jug Suraiya*

151 **Stop this futile Pak bashing** *—TK Arun*

154 **Dump opium in Afghanistan, bankrupt Taliban** *—SA Aiyar*

157 **Crown and country** *—Jug Suraiya*

159 **We don't need an Osama to destabilise us** *—Rajesh Kalra*

162 **Wimpish India may lose the Great Game** *—Swapan Dasgupta*

165 **What after the Jasmine fades?** *—Ranjan Roy*

168 **Wikileaked and scared** *—Indrani Bagchi*

Business 170

170 **Oil makes the world go round** *—Sudeshna Sen*

173 **Corruption per square foot** *—Abheek Barman*

176 **Invest, as crude prices soar** *—TK Arun*

179 **In trust deficit too, China races ahead of India** *—Abheek Barman*

Sports 181

181 **Is Sachin the greatest of all? The debate rages on** *—Bobilli Vijay Kumar*

184 **Proud to be an Indian** *—Saibal Bose*

186 **Why was Summer of 83 sweeter?** *—Raja Bose*

189 **Saina: the golden girl with nerves of steel** *—Bobilli Vijay Kumar*

Living 191

191 **Reluctant lover** *—Jug Suraiya*

193 **Lips don't lie: The Royal kiss Kate and William shared!** *—Vinita Dawra Nangia*

195 **Be good in what you do – it'll work** *—Kingshuk Mukherji*

197 **'Value for money' Premji** *—Kingshuk Nag*

200 **Buri nazar waley, terey muh par chasma** *—Kannan Somasundaram*

202 **Economics of death** *—Jug Suraiya*

204 **An everlasting love** *—Vinita Dawra Nangia*

207 **Why did this have to happen to me?** *—Kingshuk Mukherji*

Entertainment 210

210 **Do we need a censor board at all?** *—Alok Tiwari*

213 **Mard ko dard nahi hota** *—Rupam Singh Gupta*

215 **Too much tosh on sale** *—Pritish Nandy*

218 **Chul Bull Pandey!** *—Anshul Chaturvedi*

About the Bloggers 220

Preface

A government directive that led to blocking of blogs in July 2006 proved to be the turning point for the Indian blogosphere. At least 17 websites were blocked on government orders without giving any reason. Some of these sites belonged to Google's Blogspot, a leading international weblog hosting service. A trend that was slow to pick up initially in India became quite a rage after the ban sparked such a furore that many people who didn't have a clue what a blog is found all about it. Be it political, business, spirituality, Bollywood and sex, there is little that Indian bloggers don't cover these days.

"Blog" is an abbreviated version of "weblog," a term used to describe websites that maintain an ongoing chronicle of information. Blogs range from personal to political, and focus on one particular subject or a whole range of subjects. Worldwide, as in India, blogs have gained increasing popularity and coverage for their role in breaking, shaping, and spinning news stories.

Though mainly seen as partisan gossips, blogs and bloggers sometimes bring key information to public light, with mainstream media following their lead. Today, blogs are increasingly used by social activists, political leaders, sportspersons, media professionals, celebs etc, as tools for outreach and opinion forming.

Keeping pace with the times, The Times of India gives a platform, through its online service, to all to voice their opinion through blogs. The blogs are informative, educative and makes interesting read.

This book, TOI Blogs, is a compilation of blogs of noted journalists of The Times of India and columnists who have contributed to the newspaper on a regular basis. They are famous, popular and policy influencers and known for their journalistic skills.

This book has been divided into different sections ranging from topics on India, politics, world affairs, business, sports, living and entertainment. There are interesting blogs by Bachi Karkaria, who in her usual style, takes a dig at the Pulitzer prize; SA Aiyar suggests ways of preventing licensing scams in India; Jug Suraiya highlights the tragic case of Aruna Shanbaug; Shobhaa De blogs on the outcome of the recent elections where women have held centrestage; Pritish Nandy dwells on the after effects of high profile assassinations after the killing of Osama bin Laden; Ranjan Roy talks about the Jasmine Revolution going on in the Arab world; TK Arun points out ways of reforming political funding in India; Gurcharan Das eggs on the Prime Minister to speak out on the spate of scams coming out of his government; Vinita Dawra Nangia enumerates the royal wedding in Britain, Anshul Chaturvedi blogs about his visit to Pakistan and how he found it be so different from what is projected in the media; Bobilli Vijay Kumar profiles Sachin Tendulkar and his stature in world cricket; Rajesh Kalra highlights the dirty tricks played by the government to hide corruption-related issues and scams; Indrani Bagchi puts up questions for Pakistan after the death of Osama bin Laden.

This book on blogs will motivate you to sit up and take note of the developments happening in the country even if you have little or no interest in it.

Why assassinations don't work

Pritish Nandy | 09 May 2011

Only an idiot murders a political adversary. A wise man defeats him. For killing a person never destroys what he stands for. Nor the idea he embodies. On the contrary, it brings it into sharper focus and, as we have seen in the past, makes heroes out of often undeserving people. A perfect example was Bhindranwale whose followers made him a Sant the moment Indira Gandhi stormed the Golden Temple and killed him in Operation Bluestar. It was a brilliant tactical strike but a wrong political move. The outcome was years of strife and non-stop terrorism in Punjab. It ended ultimately in the assassination of Mrs Gandhi herself. Even that didn't lay the ghost of Bhindranwale. It has taken many long years of political struggle to rebuild peace in the state. In retrospect, the killing of Bhindranwale achieved nothing. It only delayed the process of reconciliation and healing.

Assassination, as Woody Allen said, is an extreme form of censorship and, as we all know, particularly those among us who write, paint or make movies, the act of censorship diminishes the censor more than the person or the work being censored. DH Lawrence has outlived the censors and is recognised as one of the greatest writers of our time. So is Salman Rushdie. In fact, every philosopher, scientist, painter, cartoonist, movie maker or journalist ever gagged, jailed or murdered has eventually survived the censors and critics. Galileo Galilei spent his entire life in prison for defying the Church and saying that the earth spun around the sun. Four centuries later, the Pope who sent him to prison has been forgotten. No one knows his name. But Stephen Hawking acknowledges Galileo as the father of modern science. So did Einstein.

That Osama misrepresented Islam and killed thousands of innocent people, including women and children, and yes many Muslims among them, is well chronicled. For most Americans, post 9/11, he was the face of evil. Even we Indians, who have not faced an Al Qaeda attack, identify him with terror, not religion. He was the man we loved to hate. Not for what he did to us. But for what he kept threatening to do. We knew Kashmir was always in his crosshairs. Every message he sent America was also a message for us. When Daniel Pearl was brutally murdered in front of the video camera and the world, it was as if one of us was killed. It was this ugly, gratuitous, inexplicable violence that eventually diminished Osama's influence, a fact that was so tellingly revealed during the recent spring in Arab nations when thousands of citizens streamed out on the streets to protest, in Egypt, Yemen, Libya, Bahrain, Syria, Algeria, Iran, Tunisia, Iraq, Morocco, Oman, Jordan, Kuwait, Lebanon, Saudi Arabia. Everyone among them spoke of freedom and a new life. Resurgent Islam was nowhere on their agenda. They didn't give a damn about the Al Qaeda.

That is why this sudden strike in Abbotabad, the killing of Osama may end up achieving the precise opposite of what America wanted. No doubt there will be some kind of emotional closure. The ghost of 9/11 will be exorcised. But who knows? Osama's legatees may benefit too, and Pakistan, the nation that secretly hosted him and cunningly used his decadent ideology of hate as an instrument of political blackmail to terrorize the world. You may even see some random terror strikes to prove that Osama may be dead, not the Al Qaeda. Rabids could emerge from secret safe houses to reassert themselves, avenge the killing of their leader, and try to reconstruct their universe of terror fast disintegrating in the face of new, emerging ideologies of hope and freedom even in the most despotic Muslim nations. That's why I believe it was a wrong move. The conspiracy theories it has spawned may help to resuscitate an ideology that was dying on its own. It would have been so much simpler to bring Osama to trial and expose his crimes. As they did with Saddam.

Murders are never popular. Especially political murders. They create a backlash, often far worse than the original crime. That's why it's important to reconsider downloading assassination as a smart app. You run the risk of working up sympathy even among those who hate the victim. It's this sympathy that morphs the most villainous among us into putative heroes. That's why the canny Mahatma said, "An eye for an eye makes the whole world blind". It wasn't just pious rhetoric. It's smart politics. The most enduring hero of our freedom struggle wasn't Bhagat Singh or Khudiram. It wasn't Sri Aurobindo or Subhash Chandra Bose. It was a man who repeatedly spoke of non violence as the most powerful weapon of our times. And, what's more important proved that again and again by his life and deeds.

He also proved by his death how stupid and meaningless assassinations are. Six decades on and there are still no takers for Nathuram Godse who tried to assert his patriotism by shooting the Mahatma with a .38 Beretta.

This blog was written after the American Navy Seals killed Osama bin Laden in his Abbottabad hideout in Pakistan on the night of 1st May 2011.

As public anger increases, corruption falls

SA Aiyar | 15 May 2011

The electoral debacle of the DMK-Congress in Tamil Nadu highlights public disgust with corruption, and underpins the Anna Hazare anti-graft crusade. But is corruption really worsening, or is the public simply angrier about it? Most survey data suggest, surprisingly, that corruption has been declining. Crooked politicians look enormously richer than ever before. Corruption has surely skyrocketed in real estate, natural resources and government contracts. But it has disappeared in deregulated areas like industrial and import licensing and foreign exchange.

Falling import duties have almost killed smuggling.

The annual corruption perception index of Transparency International (TI) gives country scores for corruption on a scale of 1 to 10, with 1 being most corrupt and 10 being least corrupt. India has gradually improved its score, from 2.78 in 1995 to 2.8 in 2000, 2.9 in 2005 and 3.3 in 2010. This is modest improvement.

In 1995, India was ranked 34th of 41 countries surveyed, near the bottom. But subsequent surveys covered many more countries, most of whom were far more corrupt than India. In 2010, India came 87th of 178 countries, halfway down the list. This is no cause for rejoicing: a score of 3.3 is pathetic when the best countries score 9. But it's a small mercy if things are getting a bit better.

In 2010, China (3.5) scored marginally more than India. Much worse were Vietnam (2.7), Pakistan (2.3) and Russia (2.1).

TI has a separate bribe payers index (BPI), measuring the

willingness of a country's businesses to pay bribes abroad. The latest list for 2008 list covers only 22 countries. The most willing to bribe abroad is Russia (5.9) followed by China (6.5), Mexico (6.6) and India (6.8). So, India is pretty bad, but not the worst. Its score has improved from 4.2 in 2006 to 6.8 in 2008, and it has overtaken China, Mexico and Russia in the process.

Ordinary Indians worry most about the small local-level corruption that extracts money directly from their pockets for services that should be free. TI surveys show that people perceive corruption to be rising in the vast majority of countries, even the most honest Scandinavian countries, and it's unclear whether such perception is mostly emotional or factual. More reliable than perceptions are data on the proportion of households who actually paid a bribe in the last year.

TI brings out a Global Corruption Barometer. This suggests that bribes paid by ordinary Indians for access to government services have shot up from 16% of households in 2003 to 54% in 2010. That sounds absolutely calamitous. But the very opposite is suggested by surveys conducted by CMS, a well respected survey organization. CMS suggests that the proportion of Indians saying they paid a bribe in the 12 months literally halved from 56% to 28% between 2005 and 2010. This looks like a fabulous outcome. Ironically, the CMS report was released by the local head of Transparency International, with no sense of the glaring contradiction between the two reports. The TI surveys have a small sample size of around 1,000 people. CMS, on the other hand, surveyed almost 9,000 people in 2005 and 10,000 in 2010, and therefore boasts a more robust statistical base. The CMS also has a more rural focus.

The CMS survey asked about bribes in relation to four government services — the public distribution system for food, education, water supply and health. The TI survey covered nine areas, including the police, courts and registry officials. Can this explain the difference in outcome of the two surveys? Not really, it is implausible that the four areas surveyed by CMS could have improved dramatically while the others surveyed by TI worsened dramatically: quality trends in administration tend to be similar across sectors.

Surveys can be contradictory. We cannot ignore the Barometer's survey. Yet the positive trends of the CMS survey are more in line with TI's corruption perception index and bribe payers index, both of which show corruption decreasing. CMS gives several possible reasons for declining bribes, such as improved technology and media activism. Nonsense, say sceptics, politicians are making unprecedented billions today. The debate will continue.

Whatever the truth, we can celebrate the CMS finding that media and TV coverage of corruption has risen fourfold in five years! This suggests a social revolution. Fast GDP growth has created a rising middle class that refuses to sit back and accept corruption as *chalta hai*. TV is amplifying this middle class anger into political change, first in Anna Hazare's coup and now in the DMK defeat. Hurrah! Let's build on this anger : we have a long way to go.

Women must seek poribartan now

Shobhaa De | 15 May 2011

Namaskaram Amma. Nomoshkaar Didi. Congratulations ladies! *Bhalo khobor!* You've done it and deserve the applause. To borrow Mayawati's words, the time for *dramabaazi* is over. You have won. The people of your respective states have given the verdict . Jai ho, and all that. Your time begins now. Showing the door to rivals is the easy part. Both of you can confidently take the oath, look and feel smug... and if you so wish, dance in the streets or on the posters of your vanquished opponents. No doubt your myriad followers will join you with abundant joy. Gloat away! But this is about your future agendas — especially those involving your own gender. What specific policies will you be working on that will benefit the women of your state, and maybe even, women across India ? Come on, you two. You can do it! Mamata has spoken eloquently about the appalling conditions faced by rural women in West Bengal. She has said she wants to create infrastructure for underprivileged pregnant women, who are forced to walk up to 15 km to deliver babies. Well, action it, Didi. Get those clinics to happen, *taara-taari*.

It cannot be a significantly better scenario in Tamil Nadu. We are also aware of the 'corporate bladder' syndrome (no loos for working women in urban India), but for how many more years will our village women have to wait for the protective cover of darkness before they can 'go' ? These may look like *chhota-mota* issues to powerful politicians in search of bigger issues to tom-tom — like attracting instant foreign investment. But please don't take women's bladders and wombs for granted ! We need clean facilities. Period. Whether it's maternity wards in which to deliver babies, or conveniently located latrines that are safe for use, day and night. This is not a tall order, but it is an urgent one. If this initiative can be announced and undertaken on a priority basis by both of you, you will win the whole-hearted support of countless deprived women who have put up with painful urinary tract infections, botched births by the roadside and other related horror stories for decades ...no, centuries.

The women of India have waited long enough. Too long. So far, their voices, their expectations, their anxieties were of zero consequence to successive governments. Much was expected from Pratibha Patil as president. Much more was hoped for from Sonia Gandhi. No miracles. No waving of magic wands. Just simple plans and projects that would have made it easier for women to hang in there and be counted. Nothing of any consequence was announced by either one of them unfortunately, and women meekly went back to the starting post to patiently begin their vigil all over again. Perhaps it's not such a good thing that our women are passive. We let off our netas a bit too easily. We make far too many concessions.

Mamata's win was largely based on *poribartan* (change). But there was little mention in her manifesto of gender-specific policies that would be beneficial to women. As the railways minister, her track record was disappointing at a time when women travellers cried out for safety on trains. Mamata's perceived indifference to the woes of women commuters was seen as being callous and shortsighted.

Ditto for Jayalalithaa, whose past record isn't exactly impressive with regards to women's issues. If anything, Amma remained aloof and indifferent when confronted. This time, she didn't bother wooing women or men, for that matter.

In fact, she didn't woo anybody! She didn't have to. Her old foes (the DMK gang led by the old war horse Karunanidhi) obliged Amma by committing hara-kiri while she romped home, without lifting a finger. Our female politicians are street smart and canny. They have been told by their minders that raising women's issues during elections is not politically wise. It alienates men! And political pundits have consistently insisted it's men who are the real game changers in any election. The big numbers are driven by men. Why bother courting women? Today, we are crowing about four important women leading four important states of India. Forget, the most important woman in the country (you-know-who). It's time to ask a few uncomfortable questions of these *chaar deviyaan.* Starting with Sheila Dikshit and Mayawati, who have been around long enough to have got things moving. But their *mahila gaadis* stalled a long time ago and refused to change gear, as these two steamrolled their way past other, more critical-to-survival obstacles, conveniently forgetting all about their less-privileged sisters.

It's a terrible fact of life, but the bitter truth is that women in politics have not leveraged their position to do anything substantial for other women. Perhaps, those vintage Ekta Kapoor serials had a point — which is why they worked. But even Ekta has moved on and away from those dreary subjects to sexier ones. Why can't our female politicians do the same? This is their chance to win the loyalty of what is, in reality, their core constituency — women. Woo us with policies that transform lives and you'll never have to worry about your warm *kursi* going to someone else. Neglect us now... and watch! Just you watch! We'll show you! Remember , there is no 'next time' in politics. Mind it!

This blog was written after the State elections in West Bengal and Tamil Nadu.

The Pillitzer Prize

Bachi Karkaria | 20 April 2011

Dr Siddhartha Mukherjee has just won the prestigious Pulitzer Prize for 'The Emperor of All Maladies', his 'elegant inquiry' into the history and continuing mystique of cancer. Wow. But, while reading about the New Delhi-born, New York-based oncologist's impressive literary achievement, it struck me that our entire news media is about maladies. And the unquestioned emperor of all these is politics.

It wasn't just a coincidence that the biggest headline of not just that day, but the whole week, was about a doctored CD, and the cancer of corruption which has been galloping unchecked across the body politic.

Serious illness means ambulance. Some lawyers are known as ambulance chasers, and there have been whispers that the Bhushans have been doing just this in the guise of public interest. Their targets make no bones about these two busybodies being a pain in the neck. Some people have an even lower opinion of them. But they have to swallow their bitter PIL.

Like the subject of Dr Mukherjee's book, the Bhushan CD continues to confound the fraternity. Everyone has made it his business to diagnose it, including those who are accused of doctoring it. Pathologist Amar Singh has asked Shanti Bhushan to give a voice sample to establish proof of his paternity. Many suspect that the former SP leader is the one who should be taking the test.

Like allopathic medicos who dismiss any form of alternative medicine as hocus poke-us, the ruling politicos have branded Homeopath Hazare as a dangerous quack who will cause severe, long-term damage to the system. They say we must ignore his bogus white pills, and leave the treatment of corruption to those with a proper MP degree.

However, alarmed by the multiple organ failure caused by this galloping cancer, more and more people are beginning to place their faith in Anna-ji's grassroots prescription. So what if he's not that kind of pharma?

Shanti and Prashant Bhushan are a father and son team. This is common practice in law. As it is in medicine. Politics is even more genetically engineered. *Biwi, bahu, beta* are all symptoms or side effects. Since even *chacha-bhanja* causal links are found, the practice of this cancer is sometimes known as Uncology.

The deep-rooted cancers of the body politic have compromised its immunity, and also made it more susceptible to external factors. The very day that Dr Siddhartha Mukherjee was chosen for the Pulitzer, in faraway Ratnagiri, virulent protests against the Jaitapur plant exposed the already ravaged government to the hazards of unclear radiation.

Political maladies manifest themselves differently at different times. Parts of the country are now in the grip of a poll fever. Following textbook epidemiology, it was preceded by a rash of campaigning, blistering allegations, and bouts of violent attacks. Medical opinion differs on the best way to get it to subside or prevent it from assuming a virulent, or even fatal, form. But most agree that the best bet not only for diagnosis, but even treatment is the EC-*ji.*

Now that it is well established that politics is the emperor of all maladies, it follows that New Delhi's biggest hospital should be headed by a Dr Singh. Several expressers of mock concern have been suggesting that the Prime Medico himself needs a good orthopaedic surgeon to tackle his apparently weak knees and spine. The more aggressive say he needs complete replacement. Hopefully it won't come to that. We might mention that here, as in all hospitals, it's the Matron who actually calls the shots.

India's racing ahead, but are we on track?

TK Arun | 04 October 2010

India is getting ready to play. The government's chief economist says India will soon overtake China as the world's fastest growing economy. So it would, concurs a Morgan Stanley study, based on the expected demographic dividend as the share of the non-working, dependent population shrinks, boosting not only the share of active workers but also the savings required to finance massive investment. Foreign direct investment inflows of the magnitude that the world envied China for, for much of the last couple of decades, is now flowing into India. Indians themselves are aggressive outward investors, and investment promotion outfits of most advanced countries woo Indian capital.

The president of the United States warns his country's children that if they don't study hard, Indian children will eat their jobs. Indian enterprise is respected, even feared, as being capable of devouring good, middle-American jobs, if business process outsourcing is not curbed.

Indian managers are making their mark around the world. Indra Nooyi, Vikram Pandit and Anshu Jain have steered their ships with great elan over the choppy waters of the financial and economic crisis, to the far shore of greater profitability. Prime Minister Manmohan Singh's views are received with respect and attention, when leaders of the world meet, to discuss globally coordinated solutions to global problems.

Yes, on most counts, India would indeed seem to be getting ready to play. So it would seem appropriate that India should host a major sporting event like the Commonwealth Games. However, the manner in which we went about organising them, producing a sordid tale of incompetence, corruption and shoddiness that has been unfolding in daily installments to public shock and horror, has made us hang our heads in shame.

But this is not all. The nation was on edge on September 30th, when a high court delivered its verdict on a disputed shrine at Ayodhya. The police forces were on full alert in all parts of the country. Several states had issued prohibitory orders, closed schools and colleges, in anticipation of violence that is no less menacing for its eventual non-occurrence. Should a nation about to take wing be cringing at its own reflection morphed through a prism of anger? The insurgencies in Kashmir and the north-east and by the Maoists, the concept of honour that impels father and brother to kill daughter and sister, the skewed distribution o social power that makes Dalits easy prey to the greed and lust of upper caste miscreant, the custom and mores that make even the Capital's Metro provide exclusive compartments for women and, every so often, send a doctor off to jail for conducting pre-natal sex determination tests, what do all these tell us about the state of the Union? If this is preparation for play, what macabre sport are we preparing for?

Yes, there is ugliness in our midst that the opening ceremony spectacle or Shera, the Games mascot's smile or the colourful screens planted strategically all along the route the foreign athletes would travel cannot conceal. But India is not just chaos and dirt and violence. If there is one thing that suffuses India's collective consciousness today as never before, it is hope — hope that things would improve, drastically, and for everyone. Without hope for the future, there can be neither joy in the present, nor creative action. But there is, indeed, hope, and joy, and plenty of action. India is indeed prepared to play. Let the games play on!

How Binayak Sen became a cause celebre

Swapan Dasgupta | 09 January 2011

At the risk of appearing to be callous or, indeed, flippant, it may be suggested that the elevation of Binayak Sen from a relatively unknown activist to a cause célèbre is partly due to a dramatic image makeover. When Sen was arrested in May 2007 by the Chhattisgarh police on charges of aiding and abetting the Maoist insurgency, the photograph of him in circulation was that of a thickly bearded stereotype of the Bengali intellectual espousing unattainable radical causes over endless cups of tea and unfiltered cigarettes.

The Sen that appeared before the public in May 2009, after the Supreme Court granted him bail on grounds of ill health, presented a striking departure. The lush beard had gone and, instead, there was the benign face of a man who had withstood two years of incarceration in inhospitable jails with fortitude. If the captions hadn't indicated this was Sen, he could have been easily mistaken for either a kindly primary school teacher or a jholawala with an NGO.

The earnestness, however, was intact. But if the pre-2007 portrait of a Bengali Che Guevara prone to reckless excitability was quaintly disturbing, the post-2009 image was distinctly nonthreatening. Like the distracted Kobad Ghandy, Doon School's contribution to the Indian revolution, the Sen that smiled and posed for photographs after being sentenced to life imprisonment seemed incapable of either malevolence or subversion. He just didn't fit the mental picture of a dangerous man.

The striking mismatch between what TV images suggested and what the sessions court judge in Raipur pronounced may help understand why the recent discourse on Sen has been so woefully one-sided. To the young and the impressionable, to cause-hungry 'intellectuals' and to NRI grandees on their winter vacation, Chhattisgarh is India's Heart of Darkness. In this imagined state, governed by the political first cousins of those who administer Gujarat, heavy-handed policing, law of the jungle, capitalist iniquity and the brutal suppression of tribal rights exist in equal measure.

"For the past several years," Sen is quoted by a PUCL pamphlet as declaiming shortly before his initial arrest, "we are seeing all over India-and, as part of that, in ... Chhattisgarh as well-a concerted programme to expropriate from the poorest people in the Indian nation their access to essentials, common property resources and to natural resources, including land and water."

It is not that Sen's perception of a "concerted programme" of expropriation is widely shared, even by those horrified by the harshness of the sentence. If Amartya Sen in his scholarly avatar is any guide, democracy is the great corrective and India is about as rumbustious a democracy as you can get. In that case, is Chhattisgarh the rotten apple?

The prevailing discourse has presented the issue as a simple war between the forces of enlightenment and darkness. Sen was the barefoot doctor who attended to the sick and needy, articulated their hopes and fears, and raised his voice against state oppression. For that he was targeted, framed and sentenced. "If the high court has its thinking straight and unbiased," declared the Nobel Prize winner Sen, "it will overturn the decision." Anything else, he argued, would imply that "as happened in Gujarat-justice is difficult to get in the state, which is under the control of a political regime that is keen on justifying its policies, some of which are very deeply problematic, rather than bringing justice to people living in Chhattisgarh...."

Such an assertion is astonishing in its arrogance. Disagreement with a judicial verdict is part of the democratic debate. But to assume that any alternative perspective implies a bent and biased system is rash. It has as much validity as Ilina Sen's outburst that state intolerance could compel dissidents to seek political asylum overseas.

Sen may or may not be an overground functionary of the Maoist underground that specializes in murder and extortion. At present, we can only go by the sessions court judgment. Yet, by leveraging the publicity surrounding his arrest and conviction, his supporters have given the Maoist insurgency unintended legitimacy. It is one thing to claim that the evidence against Sen has been planted by a vengeful police. That's a technical issue of evidence and one that the higher courts will review. But 'human rights' activists have used their anger at the judgment to turn every TV studio into not merely an appellate court but a political forum to cast aspersions on the credentials of both the criminal justice system and Indian democracy.

The right to campaign peacefully for Sen is a feature of India's open society. However, the campaign's successful creation of a paranoid discourse suggests interesting possibilities for those who have no time for the India we value and cherish.

This blog was written after Dr Binayak Sen was found guilty of waging war against India and sentenced to life term by a Chhattisgarh court on December 24, 2010.

Games a metaphor for all that's wrong with Indian democracy

CP Surendran | 16 August 2010

Who wanted the Commonwealth Games to be held in Delhi? The Indian poor, who constitute half the population, as a norm, were never consulted. But then neither were we, the wannabe middle class. As for the rich, they don't care. They might have, if it were the Olympics. The Commonwealth Games event, for all the din it is drumming up, is a second-rate sports show. Ask any Olympian.

The origin of the Indian chapter of the event, as its conduct afterwards, was oligarchical. It was devised by a few influential people; it was run on a command structure, doing away with the need for democratic procedures. These were the fault lines at the inception of the games. And they have now developed into chasms.

The Delhi games took shape at the initiative of a handful of politicians and officials. The two principal bids for the 2010 Commonwealth Games were from Delhi, India, and Hamilton, Ontario, Canada. A ballot of member nations was held in November 2003 at the Commonwealth Games Federation General Assembly in Montego Bay, Jamaica.

India shifted the balance in its favour by promising that it would provide $100,000 to each participating country, along with all expenses paid. Without this bribe, Canada would have walked away with the games. We began with a bribe. And as recent media reports show, we are likely to end with it. Payoffs are the name of the game(s).

Politicians and officials were desperate for the games. Apparently, the idea was to showcase India's rising status as an international power. The games cost roughly Rs 7,000 crore. And Rs 20,000 crore more would go into related infrastructure development of Delhi. In other words, this was an egotistical exercise, an expensive opportunity to flex the muscles of the national hubris. The fundamentally despotic nature of ego driven activities has been at the centre of the games exercise. Consider the instances of authoritarianism: This summer, school-going children of Delhi and the national capital region were deprived of their vacation by one month. The reason: so they can take 30 days off in October when the games would be on and they could be deployed as a cute army of volunteers, winning the hearts of the visitors. Neither parents, nor school authorities were consulted before the measure was taken. It was a command.

A little over Rs 744 crore was diverted from the Special Component Plan and the Scheduled Caste Sub Plan to the games funds. This was revealed in answer to an RTI request by an NGO. Funds meant for housing, education and employment of the underclass have been given to sellers of marble and concrete so Delhi looks good. This lookist obsession has been sublimated at the expense of the constituency that the funds were meant to benefit. There was no discussion in the open about the perceived necessity for such a dire diversion.

In October, a new lane on NH 8 that connects Gurgaon to Delhi will be devoted exclusively to Commonwealth Games participants, according to the games organising committee officials. The commuters who pay toll to ply the congested road and who are frequently stuck in traffic jam have not been consulted. The officials believe that the games tourists and participants should not be expected to fritter their time in traffic snarls. It's not clear why commuters who pay for their ride on the road must play second fiddle to those who are games participants or just tourists. Or why their time is less precious. There is no explanation, because this is just another command. There have been instances of hundreds of beggars and homeless of the capital being rounded up and sentenced up to three years in remand homes. Mothers and children are separated, sent to different custodial homes. These may be destitute, but surely they are Indian citizens? And surely, too, they feel pain and terror just as a million other Indians do? If beautification means the separation of the mother from the child, what is brutalization? During the Emergency years, Sanjay Gandhi displayed a similar streak in cleaning up Delhi. The games officials and the Delhi administration in general display much the same dictatorial impulse. What is at the heart of that impulse is not the angelic one of removing poverty, but the termination of the poor. It is extreme sanitation.

A similar authoritarian ideology is at work in the eviction of thousands of students from 13 hostels of Delhi University for three months. The rooms are being done up so visiting Games officials can stay at the hostels. The students were never consulted. The university was merely told. The students of DU are on a relay fast in protest.

The games were brought — and bought — on the excuse of patriotism and associated infrastructural development of Delhi. The claim to patriotism stands exposed with the corruption scandals and the rooted notion of the supplementary income as a matter of right among our politicians and bureaucrats. Patriotism has been reduced to a pretext for generating puff-money.

As for Delhi's development, it is a telling comment that the capital of an allegedly rising superpower needs the excuse of an event before it can get a few good roads and some airconditioned buses.

Clearly, the games stand as a detailed metaphor for all that's wrong with Indian democracy. Each stadium and footpath tile, swimming pool and turf is a critique of the opaque, exclusionary developmental model: 15% to you; 85% to them. And the loser gets to watch the games.

This blog was written before the 2010 Commonwealth Games held in Delhi in October.

The attack of dirty-tricks department

Rajesh Kalra | 20 April 2011

The anti-corruption movement that seemed to start with a lot of promise is now in the danger of being obliterated by the state-sponsored dirty-tricks department itself. Not that one hadn't expected this. I myself have maintained that politicians — of all hues and shapes and parties — can never accept the clauses contained in the draft, for it affects their very survival, but the ferocity of attack from all flanks on those who are spearheading the campaign is unbelievable.

The shameless manner in which the ruling party has gone about discrediting the non-political members of the committee has shocked almost everybody with a semblance of civility. I was, honestly, surprised at the ease, and alacrity, with which the government agreed to Anna Hazare's demand for a joint committee. It should, if anything, have been a dead giveaway.

The government clearly had its reasons to nip this in the bud. With a relentless media glare, Anna was fast becoming an icon that the TV-watching class, filled with angst over repeated scams, was waiting to lap up. His frequent, no-nonsense statements and sound bytes would have become increasingly difficult for the government to handle later. Of course, the crafty politicians/lawyers in the ruling class must have already thought through by then the shape this 'nipping in the bud' would take.

Instead of debating the issues in a civilised manner, in line with their reconciliatory statements to the media during the hunger strike, what started from every flank was the character assassination of some of the committee members. As Anna wrote to Sonia Gandhi a couple of days into character assassination attempts, some senior persons from the ruling party were behind the baseless allegations and it seemed that they had the party's backing. It did not stop with leaked stories to a pliable media alone, every dirty trick in the trade that would do some of the corporate houses proud, was used. To top it all, they also roped in the patron saint of "all that is good" with our politics, Amar Singh.

Without going into details, the so-called Shanti-Prashant Bhushan tape too had Singh as a protagonist and the judge they refer to is the one at the forefront of the 2G investigations. Now, the ruling party, which is currently under fire for countless scams, is not the only one hurt with this particular scam, a very prominent corporate that has close links with Singh is deeply involved too. So, for the ruling class and the affected corporate, it was like killing two birds with a single shot.

What the dirty tricks department achieved in one shot was to discredit some of the prominent faces of civil society, so that the general public once again throws up its hands in despair with the common refrain being — they are all the same. In addition, it pitted the anti-corruption icon with not the bigger protagonists who will go unnamed, but a willing Singh whose own political survival is at stake now that he is not part of any major political dispensation. And most importantly, it immediately diverted attention from the task at hand to allegations and counter-allegations. And please rest assured, if the Bhushans were to be replaced with other members in the drafting committee, they would be subjected to the same slander campaign.

When Anna, in the same letter to Sonia mentioned earlier, wrote in his blunt style that this character assassination is bad for the anti-corruption movement and that the politicians and the political members of the committee indulging in this should be careful for they themselves are at a far greater risk of being exposed than the others, several from the intelligentsia reacted saying Anna is a crybaby. It's a different matter that Anna was being naive with that threat, for he forgot that unlike most in civil society, the corrupt politicians are thick-skinned.

And this was another flank that the dirty-tricks department

unleashed — the so-called intelligentsia. While one can have differences over what all should be contained in the anti-corruption bill and also who should be part of the committee from civil society or on what basis were the members from civil society chosen, the way the hallowed 'educated' class reacted was sickening. When there was some clamour for civility in discussions, these people termed the anti-corruption movement itself as being blackmail, almost telling them that it is like the pot calling the kettle black.

The way such people manipulate opinions is amazing. It is almost as if those who do not agree with their point of view are morons. So effective are they with their campaign that I have often seen some right-thinking people change their point of view only to be seen as belonging to their exalted camp.

Anyhow, this was, as I said, expected and I expect the ferocity of attacks and counter-attacks to increase. I have seen how the slander campaign has affected some of those involved. They have spent more time this past one week in fighting off these imaginary allegations than concentrating on the task at hand. This is exactly what the dirty-tricks department wants. Tire them to an extent that they compromise and also lose the buzz among the public by then. The onus is on us, 'the right-thinking people' to ensure that we don't lose focus and provide unstinted support to those fighting for the cause. Our support and demands have to be so relentless that the corrupt tire themselves out.

Lokpal not enough, we need radical reform

SA Aiyar | 24 April 2011

I wondered in this column some years ago why top businessmen were frequently prosecuted and convicted in the US but not in India. Answer: crooked politicians had mangled the police-judicial system such that it could never convict them beyond all appeals, and obviously such a moribund system could not convict crooked businessmen either. Solution: only if the system allowed crooked politicians to be nabbed would crooked businessmen be nabbed too.

I feel vindicated — and delighted — to see first politicians and then businessmen arrested in the 2G telecom scam. A very powerful telecom minister, A Raja, was first sacked and then arrested. So were top business honchos of Anil Ambani's group, Swan Telecom and Unitech. Remarkably, the CBI has even raided the office of Karunanidhi's daughter, Kanimozhi, once viewed as too powerful to touch. She was raided although it was politically an ultra-sensitive time (during an election campaign), and the raid could be the final nail in the ruling coalition's coffin.

But don't assume that those arrested will actually be convicted, or that it will produce clean politics and business. That did not happen in earlier corruption scams that shook the country. The anti-corruption campaign of Jayaprakash Narayan in 1974-75 toppled the Chimanbhai Patel government in Gujarat and contributed to Indira Gandhi's defeat in the 1977 general election, yet within a few years both politicians were back in power unscathed.

In 1989, voters ousted Rajiv Gandhi because of the Bofors scam, yet this did not lead to any convictions beyond appeals, and one of the accused — Win Chadha — died of old age. Something similar happened in the Jain hawala scam of the 1990s, entailing payments to politicians across the political spectrum. The political class stalled investigation, but then the Supreme Court ordered the CBI to investigate and prosecute. Alas, this was done in such slipshod fashion — because of political pressure — that nobody was convicted beyond appeals.

Will a similar fate befall the latest anti-corruption movement, starting with middle-class rage over the Commonwealth Games and culminating in Anna Hazare's campaign for a Lokpal (ombudsman) with real teeth? True, the CBI has gone after powerful politicians like Raja and Kanimozhi, yet they are not more powerful than those that emerged unscathed in the Jain hawala case (LK Advani, Madhavrao Scindia, VC Shukla, Sharad Yadav, Shiv Shankar and others).

Nor is it clear that the evidence gathered so far in the 2G scam is any stronger than in the hawala case. The CBI has traced a payment of Rs 200 crore to Kanimozhi's Kalaignar TV, but the company says this was an inter-corporate loan that was later repaid. Anyway, Rs 200 crore is tiny compared with the supposed scam size of over Rs 50,000 crore.

Maybe stronger evidence will turn up as the case proceeds, but even that may not be a clincher. Remember Sukh Ram, telecom minister in 1991-96? After his party was beaten in the 1996 election, the United Front government raided his house and caught him red-handed with crores in cash, stuffed into suitcases or wrapped in bedsheets.

But it took no less than 13 years for the courts to pronounce him guilty, and impose a very light sentence of three years imprisonment. Sukh Ram has appealed against the verdict. He is 84 years old and looks certain to die of old age before exhausting all appeals.

Given this history, don't expect too much of the CBI in the 2G scam case. And don't get too excited about the Lokpal Bill because even a strong Lokpal's decisions can be appealed to higher courts, which are dogged by long delays.

A Lokpal is not enough. We need a major overhaul of the police-prosecutor-judicial system. There is no space in this column to go into the issues involved, but without this the 2G scam will peter out like so many before it.

That apart, we need self-cleaning systems that automatically reduce corruption in the first place. One such, which I have long advocated, is a law providing that all criminal cases against elected legislators at the state or central level should get judicial priority over all other, and be disposed of within two years.

Today, many crooks enter the legislatures to stall cases they face. But once electoral victory means that their cases automatically get top priority over all others, crooks will keep out of elections altogether — electoral victory will accelerate rather than stall their legal headaches.

We cannot depend on occasional movements of the Jayaprakash Narayan or Anna Hazare sort to check corruption. The Lokpal Bill can be no more than a start towards clean politics. We need radical police-judicial reform and self-cleaning laws.

Mahatma a 'gay' icon? Why not?

Shobhaa De | 03 April 2011

Come on, India. Grow up! If the Great Soul was indeed attracted to another man, is that so hard to accept or understand? Which century are we living in? This column is being written on April Fool's Day. We are looking like the biggest fools on earth right now. One can expect bachelor boy Narendra Modi to instantly cash in on the 'sentiments' of the people of his state and ban the controversial book after dubbing it 'perverse'. Paradoxically enough, those same people are free to visit the Sabarmati Ashram in Ahmedabad and read those 'perverse' letters for themselves. I wonder how many people from Modi's city bother to go to the ashram in the first place, forget about examining the many Gandhi volumes that it houses. Yes, the same archival material used by the author (Joseph Lelyveld) for the book "Great Soul: Mahatma Gandhi and His Struggle with India."

The biggest slap in the face has come from Gandhiji's own - his grandson Rajmohan Gandhi, and great-grandson Tushar Gandhi, both of whom have described the ban as 'un-Gandhian.' Any sensible policymaker would let it go at that. And chances are the book will find its own level, its own takers and detractors, as should happen in a democracy. By attempting to suppress it, the one fallout will be this — "Great Soul" will register even greater sales! Censorship is always counterproductive — the more you suppress, the higher the curiosity. We saw that with the James Laine book on Shivaji (thank you Supreme Court, for showing better sense than the government of

Maharashtra). We shall see the same happening with this book as well. But, hello! Who can think of reading a red-hot book, when the collective focus of the country is on the red-hot game of cricket?

Let's face it, what's the single most startling disclosure in the book? That the author has claimed our revered Mahatma (and perhaps the world's most famous, self-declared celibate) had a long-term relationship with a German-Jewish architect and body builder called Hermann Kallenbach? Which makes Kallenbach, not Kasturba, the great love of his life! So? Since this 'juicy' tidbit was carried in nearly all the mainstream newspapers in India, it has been met with a rather tepid reaction that may surprise the more conservative elements of our society. "Really? Interesting!" said a slightly bored 20-year-old reading the news, before turning away. That was it. No rioting on the streets. No demand to ban the book. No baying for Lelyveld's blood. We have grown up! That is the best news ever! Today, homosexuality is no longer a taboo subject and is out there, along with other aspects of sex. Whether Gandhiji's subsequent 'experiments' with various truths were a part of his mission to come to terms with his own inclinations will remain a topic for future historians to tackle. But, according to this well-researched book (Lelyveld has based his work on material that is easily accessible, and quotes from "The Collected Works of Mahatma Gandhi" – supplementary volume 5 from the archives at the Sabarmati Ashram in Ahmedabad) there are several controversial nuggets that suggest Gandhiji was indeed in a relationship of sorts with Kallenbach, with whom he shared a home for two years. He quotes from one of Gandhiji's letters to Hermann, in which he confesses, "How completely you have taken possession of my body. This is slavery with a vengeance." A reader is free to interpret those passionate lines any which way and even disregard sexual implications when Gandhiji jokingly refers to himself as "Upper House" and Kallenbach as "Lower House".

I have yet to read the book, but I would think an author with such impressive credentials would have done his homework scrupulously before going into print. In any case, Gandhiji's sexuality has always been a subject of such complexity and debate that one more tome shouldn't matter. Unless, of course, some overzealous politician with nothing better to do, decides to make an issue out of it. Whether the

Mahatma preferred men over women is nobody's business but his. We in India have such idiotic standards when it comes to sex. If Gandhiji wrote, "I cannot imagine a thing as ugly as the intercourse of men and women," he is entitled to his opinion.

So, it's best we keep scholars, intellectuals and academics out of this. And please, let's also leave out his great-grandchildren, assorted grandnephews, grandnieces and other descendants. Nobody can possibly speak on behalf of the Mahatma and 'clarify' anything. It's not necessary, either! There is this book and no doubt, there will be many more in the future. Nothing can take away from Gandhiji's greatness, least of all his love for another man. It's amusing to read Gandhian scholar Tridip Suhrud's 'defence' of the Mahatma, in which he says, "In the late 19th and early 20th century, men addressed each other in a way that can be construed now as lovers." That's pretty twee. Who needs such justifications? Suhrud also explains that the two had "a deep bond that borders on attraction of the platonic kind." Okay, buddy. If you say so.

Let's hope whatever it was that Gandhiji shared with Kallenbach brought joy and fulfillment to their lives. Gandhiji as a gay icon? Why not? I think that's pretty cool! Perhaps it will drive young Indians to read more about the man who altered their destiny and gave India freedom.

This blog was written after the release of Joseph Lelyveld's book "Great Soul: Mahatma Gandhi and his struggle with India", which created a controversy in India.

Khadi or Teflon? Your choice

Pritish Nandy | 19 April 2011

The nation is split in two. There are those who believe change is a possibility and must be supported at any cost, setting aside cynicism. So they go on marches, light candles, join fasts, and come out into the open against corruption and venality, knowing that in a society like ours there is always a price to be paid for dissent.

On the other hand, you have those basking in the eternal sunshine of the status quo. They are the privileged ones who back current power equations for they fear that change could subvert their cosy, comfortable world of give and take. They see the Hope brigade as a bunch of political upstarts anxious to break the queue. For them, men like Anna Hazare are dangerous. If he can emerge from nowhere, with no money, no patronage, no political party to back him, and yet win the support of millions of people, how will the status quo survive? What also disturbs them is that those who have set aside cynicism to raise the banner of hope are also spurning the typical political alignments of the past. They can't be labelled any more.

So who are these new enemies of the State? No, they are not secret armies of the saffron Right. All attempts to prove that Anna Hazare has clandestine links with the RSS and the BJP have been laughed away. Nor can they be labelled, like Binayak Sen, as the ugly face of the radical Left. From a dangerous Naxalite, Sen has now cheerfully morphed into a new middle class hero after the Supreme Court sternly ticked off the State Government and set him free on bail. So who are these new *Andolan* junkies and what do they want to do? Stop all development? Subvert democracy? Derail our Parliamentary process? Hijack the political agenda? Or are they just dangerous blackmailers trying to sell us nonsensical ideas about social justice?

The argument of the cynics is simple. Where in the world has a nation progressed without corruption? Is the US graft-free? In fact, it has institutionalised graft and made lobbying on Capitol Hill a respectable profession. Is China graft-free? Go try and do business there. You will figure. Is Russia graft-free? Brazil? South Africa? If the other BRICS nations are not graft-free, why are we so anxious to sacrifice our scorching growth rate, our economic well being for such ridiculous and obsolete ideas that Anna Hazare stands for? You seriously expect a khadi clad, topiwallah, 72 year old Gandhian who has suddenly emerged from political obscurity to lead India into the 21st century? Whatever happened to our dream of building the new temples of modern India that Pandit Nehru dreamt of. What about more SEZs, more factories, better jobs, higher wages, the new lifestyle we dreamt of? Why should India's progress be waylaid by these bandits questioning our short cut to wealth?

There is an entire constituency out there, led by those who benefit from being in power or close to it, who have suddenly emerged as the great defenders of the faith. They are the cynical backbone of the power elite, who want the status quo to continue. It gives them a sense of comfort to know that things will not change in a nation where every year dollar billionaires keep growing as fast as millions slide below the poverty line. There are more people buying cars in India today than anywhere else. There are more people buying second homes. There are more tall towers coming up in our cities to taunt the homeless. Swiss banks hold more hot money from this subcontinent than from anywhere else. We even have a Chief Economic Adviser who has put up a paper on the Finance Ministry website proposing that paying bribes be made legal. Suddenly, out of nowhere, a ragtag bunch of civil society activists have emerged to question the morality of the economic model that promises us a 9.8% GDP growth.

How can all this progress be sacrificed on the altar of some stupid, old fashioned notions of morality? Can khadi take over from teflon? Will the Gandhi topi come back to mock a generation that has grown up on twitter and facebook? Are we going to sacrifice all our achievements for the sake of few crackpots chanting Vande Mataram at Jantar Mantar? For those who love the status quo, it's a clear No.

What impresses me, however, is that the main propagandists for change are the young. I see it wherever I go. Never was it more obvious than at Hazare's fast. The people queueing up behind the new heroes of our time are mostly young. The generation that drives the new social media have campaigned with greater fervour and far less cynicism than traditional media. They are the ones most excited by the promise of change. It's now up to each one of us to decide on which side we are. With the good guys struggling to bring in change? Or with the bad guys resisting it?

Kaun Banega Corruptpati?

Bachi Karkaria | 13 April 2011

Anna-ji, *Hazare saal jiyo*. You waved the magician's wand, and dared to say 'Jantar Mantar Chhoo' to the corruption that has swamped and strangulated us.

May the non-force be with you. And may the sips of juice you took that momentous Saturday squeeze out the institutionalised evil that has shamed our fair land, diluted the growth story and resulted in the global cooling towards our much-touted achievements. Well, you have unleashed a climate change on that score, and we must hail it. Heartily.

Look Pal, I'm not going to join the gripes over your Jan Lokpal Bill or make a case in defence of that too-clever Kapil Sibal who seems to be annoying you even more than the beat cop's hafta. No, sir, I have no quarrel with your crusade. My problem is with some of those who have leapt on to your platform. Swamis and sants who are neither, and several others who may wax eloquent on morality, but whose own personal ethics are on the wane. If not quite eclipsed.

A cause is known by the company it keeps, so, Anna-bhau, may I humbly suggest that, for the next stage of your war, you slash your friends as firmly as you do your foes. By all accounts, you have a groundswell of support, so you can well do without those who have jumped on to your brandwagon and could destabilise it with their own deadweight.

You have been the Anna-data, feeding our hopes for a clean society. Old cynics like me may doubt if any amount of deterrent can scrub away the long-ruling mantra of *daag achcha hai*. We may deserve to go down the drain with all that mucky water, but since you are a man of homespun and unfamiliar with trendy table thumping, may I also caution you against your cause getting tagged with a designer label. Methinks it already has been appropriated by our celebrated passionista fashionistas. Those who keep the white kurta always handy. One sigh fits all.

'Teleindignation' is its most stylish garb. Night after night, they ramp up the news channels. With the obligatory set-jaw-clenched-paw look, the sleek panellists hold forth on whatever is the platitude du jour. They work themselves up into a lather against the *daag* of the day — from murdered women to murdered democracy. In recent months, the groaning banquet of scams has so obligingly triggered the greatest feeding frenzy. The same ones which led to your gobsmacking — and slob-slapping — Hazare Effect.

But, Anna-ji, how many of your self-righteous celeb supporters are entitled to throw the first stone? Never jumped a signal and bribed the cop who jumps out from behind it? Never taken an out-of-turn or undue allotment? Never wanted a balcony illegally covered or tax dodged? And done so, *bindaas*, knowing that they could manage it with money or political influence? Maybe the watchdog should start by barking at its own door.

What worries me even more than the old hacks is the young packs who turned the "li'l ol' man in a *topi*" into their icon. With imagination fired on all cylinders, Jeans Next seized Anna Hazare's cause and made it viral. But how much of the rage burned simply because it seemed so 'cool', because they'd seen and heard how now globally 'power flows from the barrel of a Facebook'?

Long ago, Mao had also warned that Revolution is not a tea party. It needs reminding that it's much less a tee slogan. There may have been a seductive scent of Jasmine in the Delhi Spring, but Jantar Mantar wasn't quite Tahrir Square in a Gandhi *topi*.

* * *

Alec Smart said: "What's the favourite movie of Hazare's detractors? Kill Bill."

War is like an ageing actress...

Robin David | 10 May 2011

The world's most famous war photographer, Robert Capa, once said war was like an ageing actress — more and more dangerous and less and less photogenic. Fifty-seven years after Capa stepped on a mine in Vietnam and died, his words seem true even today given the manner in which the American government is hesitating to release photographs of Osama bin Laden's body.

Photographs of war have, in fact, always shaken the American conscience. Some of these photographers, who have walked the frontlines of the most violent wars of the last 100 years, have even been elevated to the status of pacifists and have been credited with showing the ugly face of war without its romanticism. The likes of Capa, David Douglas Duncan and W Eugene Smith (although it is not fair to dub Smith as just a war photographer) were also my personal favourites. I admired their courage even when others called them adrenaline junkies.

American writer and intellectual Susan Sontag paid rich tributes to war photographers in her seminal essays, 'On photography'. She wrote, "Photographs like the one that made the front page of most newspapers in the world in 1972 — a naked South Vietnamese child just sprayed with American napalm, running down the highway toward the camera, her arms open, screaming with pain — probably did more to increase the public revulsion against the war than a hundred hours of televised barbarities."

Sontag went on to add that the American public would not have accepted the Korean War between 1950 and 1953 with such ease had there been more photographs of daily life in Pyongyang.

But then, over time, cameras became so technologically advanced, they could capture every small detail of the battlefield. Images of action were no longer blurred, black-and-white pictures in which you could barely make out the outline of the fighting men. Images were now sharp and in colour allowing the viewer to study in depth the wound of a soldier whose face has been blown up by shrapnel. Blood was no longer a black trickle, trailing behind a dead body. It was dark red. It was hair-raising.

With this, the debate shifted from the legitimacy of war to what could and could not be printed. People started wondering about war's photogenic qualities. After looking at a gory picture from the battlefield, they seemed more concerned with the image of the war than the war itself.

As an amateur, I first picked up a camera in 1991, totally oblivious of the ethical issues that surround image-making. That same year a British newspaper carried the picture of the charred remains of an Iraqi soldier, burnt alive inside his own vehicle just before the cease-fire in the first Gulf War. The photograph by Ken Jarecke showed the gore of war in one powerful image, but publishing it was considered in bad taste by many. The photo is available on the Net and viewing it does require a strong stomach.

In 2009, Associated Press released a photo by Julie Jacobson, which showed a fatally wounded US marine in Afghanistan being tended to by other marines. The US defence secretary wrote a letter to AP's CEO saying it was against common decency as both the government and the family of the dead soldier had requested them not to release the photograph. The US even tried to ban such images after the controversy.

And now, the bin Laden controversy where the US feels pictures of the world's most wanted man's dead body would be used to incite more violence.

Technology aided by some good research, had two other impacts on war photography — first it demystified some war photographers, and secondly it helped detect images that had been unfairly manipulated to make them more dramatic and saleable.

Capa, for instance, lost some of his glowing halo in 2008, when it was reported that he may have cheated in getting his most famous image — a soldier is photographed at just the moment he is shot and about to fall during the Spanish Civil War in 1936. Researchers said Capa was making the soldier pose defiantly for him when he was spotted by the enemy and shot. In effect, Capa may have been responsible for the soldier's death. He was not lucky to be at the right time at the right place, as believed. I did some of my own research then and found out that fakery was not new to war photography and dated back to the American Civil War.

In more recent years, there is the famous Adnan Hajj case. A freelance photographer from Lebanon, he trained his lens on the 2006 conflict with Israel and was accused of digitally altering at least three photographs, either by adding more smoke to the scene or adding more flares than originally fired from an F-16 fighter.

Although, I don't know what disturbs me more — governments wanting only sanitised images of an increasingly violent world, or war photographers losing their hero status.

This blog was written when people all over the world were waiting to have a glimpse of Osama's dead body. There were stories doing the rounds of whether the US should release his pictures at all.

The triumph in the tragedy of Aruna Shanbaug

Jug Suraiya | 14 March 2011

Who or what is your spirit, and who owns it? Does your spirit belong to you or to your government, your religion, your society, your family? Can what you call your spirit belong to anyone, be owned by anyone, including you yourself?

These are some of the questions which — together with a thicket of thorny legal, political, social and ethical issues — will once again crop up in the aftermath of the Supreme Court ruling in the case of Aruna Shanbaug, victim of a violent rape who has been in a 'vegetative state' since 1973 when she was viciously assaulted. The court ruled that while Aruna will remain on life-support under the care of the staff of Mumbai's King Edward Memorial Hospital, others who are terminally and irreversibly ill, or in a permanent vegetative state (PVS) can now legally be allowed 'passive euthanasia' through the stopping of medication and by being taken off respiratory and other life sustaining machines. Going further, the apex court has also urged the government to decriminalise attempted suicide. Currently, an attempt to commit suicide is a punishable offence, a profoundly ironic paradox — I should be further penalised because I already find my life so unbearable that I try to end it — which suggests that the law is not just an ass but an ass with a particularly black sense of humour.

The most commonly advanced argument against permitting assisted suicide in any form — with or without the subject's consent

— is that it would lead to murderous misuse, particularly where the inheritance of property and wealth plays a motivating role. This is not just a reasonable but a vitally necessary contention. Murder, no matter how it disguises itself as mercy killing (which is what euthanasia means), cannot be an accepted part of any civilised society.

But what if I — in full command of my mental faculties — decide to put an end to my physical suffering, which I've been told cannot be cured, and ask for assistance to bring my life to a close? Such assistance is illegal, not just in India but in the great majority of countries.

The moral reason given is that as we cannot create life, including our own life, we cannot take away life. However, governments do sanction wars in which lives, including those of non-combatants, are taken away. Moreover, many governments, including the government of India, exercise the right to impose the death penalty for serious crimes. How is it morally justifiable for my government to have my life taken away in a war, or through the imposition of capital punishment, when it is orally and legally impermissible for me to seek a non-violent termination to my own existence?

The crux of this anomaly is that my life — your life — belongs not to me — or yours to you — but to the state. Or to the religion I subscribe to, or the society I live in. While in my day-to-day activities I am rightly obliged to follow the rules and regulations laid down by the state, by my religion and my society, can those rules be such as to form a cage for what for want of a better word I call my spirit, my consciousness? Without the innate freedom of consciousness — unbounded by geographical or political frontiers, or distinctions of creed and race — we wouldn't be humans but humanoids, robots without the ghost in the machine that we call the spirit, or the soul.

Consciousness, spirit, soul, call it what we will is not a possession — like a house, or a car — and cannot be owned by an abstract entity such as the state, or a religion. Indeed it cannot even be owned by that artificial construct that we call the ego. It is, essentially, freedom. It is this freedom of consciousness that makes us humans, and not automatons or vegetative organisms on a life-support system.

Don't cry for Aruna Shanbaug. That part of her that made her a conscious being, made her who she was, has long gone. The part of her which is left can be ruled over by courts of law, or tended to as a purely biological entity, a plant or a shrub, by the kind but misguided ministrations of doctors and nurses who keep her body in unhuman bondage.

No assisted suicide for her? Of course not. Suicide, of any kind, means the ending of a life. Aruna's life, in the real sense of the term, is no longer there. No one owns it. No one ever did. That is the ultimate triumph in the tragedy of Aruna.

This blog was written after Supreme Court rejected Aruna Shanbaug's plea where her counsel had pleaded for mercy killing on 7th March 2011.

There's a Pakistan beyond the ISI and terror; wish it was stronger

Anshul Chaturvedi | 26 April 2011

General VP Malik's book, "Kargil — From Surprise To Victory" is not quite what I expected to see on the shelf at the bookstore in the Sheraton lobby in Karachi; but then, after Katrina staring at me from hoardings extolling the virtues of Lux body wash and Veet hair remover, and an improbably rosy-cheeked Kareena pitching in for Head and Shoulder from her billboards, after seeing skimpily dressed babes walking the ramp on a fashion channel on one TV screen while an IPL match plays on the other in the hotel gym, after reading on the front page of The News that the Chairman US Joint Chiefs Of Staff has 'repeated the allegation' that elements of the Inter-Servies Intelligence are supporting the Sirajuddin Haqqani network — well, I am not sure what I should be expecting to see anymore. For those of us bound by the prisms of projection, a first person perspective of Pakistan is engaging, even refreshing.

I usually smirked when I read stuff along the lines of how people in Pakistan are generally friendly, even warm, towards visitors from India, that it's difficult to find traces of our inter-state animosity in everyday interpersonal behaviour. Now, I have to admit, even if it may be applicable primarily to the English-speaking class, there is more than a little truth to that opinion.

The people one meets with go out of their way to make you feel comfortable, perhaps sensing the edgy tentativeness of someone who's in Pakistan for the first time. There's very little of the hardline mindset, at least very little you can make out. Over dinner, alcohol flows freely, and on occasions the paradox is that me, the solitary "non Muslim foreigner" — the only category that can order liquor officially, as the footnote at the end of the card detailing the price of rum, whisky etc tells me in the hotel room — is the only one not with a drink in hand over extended conversation on dualities, contradictions and hypocrisy in modern day Pakistan. "There's a thriving gay culture, but that's not the sort of thing that's written about in the media here, at least not yet," you hear while everyone nods in agreement.

Young people have fairly sharp political views. "Zia-ul-Haq destroyed what we could have become and took us to where we are today," a 20-something says, before explaining why the way Pakistan's moved in the past few years has been so different from India. "You can't keep asking a country for money all the time and then ask it to keep off your affairs, it doesn't work that way", says another, while reading the latest headlines over the government's latest protest to the US. There's a smart sense of humour over things that can perhaps only be laughed at. Sample this: Why is the Pakistan Military Academy an institution superior to Harvard? Because while Harvard makes you good enough to run MNCs, passing out of PMA makes you capable of running anything at all, from railways to water to power corporations.

There's no animosity over the inequality of soft power; "Meera can't be a Shilpa, there's no way you can compare Lollywood to Bollywood", one hears when wondering if the Pakistani actress was quite in shape to be the showstopper for JJ Valaya's show at Karachi's recently held Bridal Couture Week. While I was there, news of Moin Akhtar passing away leads to many genuinely upset people, and recollections of him being described as the most versatile comic actor in the subcontinent. Then an enthusiastic journalist reminds me of something which apparently Amitabh Bachchan had said, about India never being able to have Nusrat Fateh Ali Khan, Noorjehan and Moin, to which Akhtar responded by saying how Pakistan could never have the Taj Mahal, Lata and Bachchan himself. The specific accuracy of the exchange is grey, the episode having happened many years ago, but the sentiment of mutual appreciation for the icons of our societies comes through, direct and uncomplicated. Bollywood is, and remains, India's primary representative, to the point that even when I ring the cab driver's number, his caller tune loudly rings out, '*Tere jaisa yaar kahaan, kahaan aisa yaarana...*'

We are all cynical about the doves when it comes to the Pakistani establishment, but many Pakistani people are not just unaffected by the hostile legacy, they are positively warm to India and things Indian. They also understand the implications of the radicalization of their motherland, observe that Jinnah's pictures in government buildings have quietly gone from western suit clad to more Islamic apparel over the years, and sometimes, express their sentiments in T-shirt slogans that say 'We are peace loving Pakistanis'. Despite that, why the sentiment doesn't reflect too often in Indo-Pak relations is, in hindsight, a factor of how much the official establishment on the one hand and the fundamentalist fringe on the other overshadows the middle/upper middle class in terms of ability to influence change.

A random fact to illustrate this, perhaps: the five Indians who make it to the TIME list of the 100 most influential people in the world this year are the cricket captain, a social activist, a professor of neurosciences and two mega-entrepreneurs; the sole Pakistani representative in the list is, appropriately enough, the convergence point of the establishment and the fundamentalists — the ISI chief.

Reforming political funding

TK Arun | 25 February 2011

It is welcome that the government has committed itself to reform political funding. But the thinking, in terms of state funding of elections, is flawed. The basic goal in political funding reform should be to achieve complete transparency as to how much parties and politicians spend and how they finance that spending. Reform of political funding is necessary, even if not sufficient, to tackle corruption.

Indian democracy is funded by corruption. Politicians take money out of the exchequer, sell patronage and extort money, all in the name of mobilising funds for political activity. They pocket a large part of the collection and pass on the rest to the party and the workers they employ. Since civil servants must collude for misuse of state power, this method of mobilising political funds suborns the bureaucracy and procedural hurdles proliferate as rentseeking opportunities. All the scams rocking the country have this common root.

Finding a new source of political funding away from corruption will not guarantee an automatic end to corruption – that is not the argument. But that will enable non-corrupt politicians and civil servants to fight corruption. All democracies make this traverse from very corrupt to less corrupt ways of conducting public life. The time, it would appear, has come for India to clean up its act on political funding. But precisely how do we go about this? State funding of elections is not the answer.

Politics is not just elections. A political party has to keep functioning inbetween elections, its leaders keep travelling, its offices run, its full-time workers have to be paid, its meetings, conventions, etc cost money. All this cannot be funded by the state. For the state to try and fund even a portion of the election expenses of recognised political parties would discriminate against new entrants and restrict competition.

Parties can mobilise funds from patrons and wellwishers, but should make that information public. When Sarojini Naidu famously said that it cost the party (the Congress) a fortune to keep Gandhi in poverty, she was setting up a case study on political funding.

Everyone knows that industrialists like GD Birla funded the Congress and the national movement. But it is not clear that they received proper receipts for the money they gave and that the Congress maintained detailed accounts of how precisely they spent the money. This tradition continued after Independence, of industrialists funnelling money to political parties without formal acknowledgement and of parties spending the money without detailed accounting. The difference is that if the purpose was, earlier, to keep one Gandhi in poverty, the money is now used to keep an entire tribe in obscene luxury and insatiable greed.

Political expenditure has to be monitored from the ground up. In every locality, explicit political activity can be recorded on a website, backed with photographs from ubiquitous cell phone cameras. Every party or politician must record, alongside, how much was spent on that activity and where that money came from. This must be open to scrutiny and challenge by rival political parties and voluntary watchdog groups. These locality level figures can then be aggregated at a hierarchy of higher levels, along with activity, expenditure and source of funds at each level, all the way up to the national level.

Each party and politician should be required to account for every paisa they spend or accumulate. At present, only contributions above RS 20,000 are required to be made by cheque. Modern information technology can be deployed to ensure the traceability of every rupee contributed to a party/politician.

One can think of mobile phone-like hand-held devices connected to the telecom network in the hands of tens of thousands of party workers across the country, for recording even small contributions from individually identified donors. A receipt printed out on the device could automatically be recorded at the party's website and at a central monitoring agency's website as well.

Unrecorded contributions can still be spent on unrecorded activity, of course, but competitive politics should bring to light all such activity, forcing parties to reveal its financing as well. This will raise the cost of collecting money initially, but the benefit would far outweigh the cost. The government can place a bulk order for these devices to achieve economies of scale and then selling them on to parties.

The present ridiculous ceilings on campaign expenditure must be scrapped, not raised. With transparency achieved, public suspicion of excessive money power would cap campaign expenditure where it should be. A central monitoring authority, an expanded and empowered Election Commission, for example, could monitor such claims of expenditure and income, scrutiny, challenge and defence, and reach legally binding conclusions.

For this, we need a new law to regulate political parties. We do have laws to regulate trade unions, voluntary organisations, etc but not for political parties. The law should ensure internal elections, audit of accounts, etc. Industry must realise that it is in its collective interest to clean up political funding and make all contributions by cheque. The finance minister can, perhaps, double the deduction allowed for tax purposes, from the present 100% of the contribution. Company accounts are audited, for the common good. So must political party accounts. This is entirely doable, with some political will.

Those who allowed pilots with fake licences should be tried for attempt to murder

Rajesh Kalra | 28 March 2011

Our benighted land of scams is these days witnessing a brand new addition to the ever-growing list – fake pilots. Airline after airline is discovering pilots, flying huge jets with thousands of unsuspecting passengers, without being qualified to do so.

The lid was blown off the scam when one of the largest and fastest growing airlines which recently ordered the largest number of jets from Airbus, realised that its woman pilot touched down on the tarmac a passenger-loaded airplane, on its nose wheel. The aircraft normally lands on its rear set of wheels and then the nose lowers down gently as it rolls on the tarmac. Turns out, the pilot had got the job based on a fake licence, or fake marksheet or both.

It was as if someone had opened the floodgates. Soon, other airlines realised they couldn't afford to point fingers at anyone, for all of them found themselves afflicted by the same malaise.

The civil aviation ministry and its wing to look after air safety – Directorate General of Civil Aviation (DGCA) – have been quick to denounce the 'discovery' and have promised the 'strictest' possible action against the erring airlines and pilots. Some may consider this sacking laughable, but to me it is infuriating, more so after we realised how these fake pilots have been playing with the lives of thousands of flyers every day with complete connivance of the very people who are there to ensure that they don't.

Our TV channel Times Now recently exposed a scary nexus between an aviation academy based in Baramati, Maharashtra, and senior officials of the DGCA. The academy — Carver Flying Institute has backing from top Maharashtra politicians. For the record, Baramati is the constituency of politician and union minister Sharad Pawar while the civil aviation ministry, till very recently, was run by Pawar's right-hand man, Praful Patel.

The channel expose showed how the academy continued to function despite losing its licence even as the unholy politician-DGCA top brass nexus helped untrained and ineligible pilots clear their exams so that they could ferry unsuspecting passengers. Apparently surprise inspections too were carried out at the academy with the crooked babus at DGCA ensuring the surprise element is maintained by informing the academy about it 20 days in advance.

We have heard that the government is sacking/taking action against those involved that includes the DGCA officials, the pilots and perhaps the airlines as well. This is absolutely unadulterated balderdash. What good does sacking a corrupt babu or pilot achieve in this case? ZILCH! These people have toyed with the lives of thousands. This is nothing short of an attempt to murder and they need to be booked under laws that are appropriate under the circumstances, no less.

So far we have been witnessing financial frauds being perpetuated on us. They are bad, no doubt, but they don't endanger human lives the way this pathetic and scary nexus of corrupt babus, politicians and big airlines does.

And in my view, the fake pilots would be the lowest in terms of culpability. They are desperate for jobs and in a nation where everything is available for a price, they simply want a shortcut without either being qualified or being incapable of performing the job. The real culprits are the babus and the politicians who not just allowed, but actively participated in perpetuating this attempt at mass murder. They are worse than the criminals who roam the streets.

The Indian apex court is currently in an activist mode. I would somehow wish it took cognizance of these incidents too. Not just me, but anyone would agree that the government that is itself responsible for this fraud on its people cannot be trusted with stemming this rot.

And while I am at it, let me extol all of you who feel for the nation to join Anna Hazare on April 5 as he starts an indefinite fast for demanding a people's anti-corruption law.

How to prevent licensing scams

SA Aiyar | 12 December 2010

Governments should govern. When misgovernance is exposed, as in the 2G spectrum scam, remedial action should follow. Yet we are seeing theatre parading as principle.

A rowdy opposition has paralyzed the current Lok Sabha session. Opposition parties insist that they will let the Lok Sabha function only if a joint parliamentary committee is appointed to probe the telecom 2G licences scam. The government has refused, and instead appointed a one-man inquiry committee. Because of the deadlock, Parliament has not functioned at all for 21 days.

The Times of India has calculated that the cost of a Parliament session is Rs 7.8 crore per day. In that case, the non-functioning of Parliament this session has already amounted to a Rs 164-crore scam. Whether or not former telecom minister A Raja will be found guilty in the telecom scam remains to be seen. But all political parties are dead guilty of the Rs 164-crore scam of paralyzing Parliament-this is a scandalous misuse of taxpayer's money.

Congress worthies sanctimoniously blame opposition rowdies for sabotaging Parliament. Yet the Congress, no less than the opposition, is engaged in political theatre. If the Congress were serious, it would simply ask Speaker Meira Kumar — an old Congress hand — to suspend the rowdies and let the others continue with normal legislative business. This is indeed what used to happen in the Nehruvian era.

But not anymore. The Congress itself resorts to the same disruptive tactics when it is in opposition. So, all parties have come to a disgraceful, unwritten agreement that the right to paralyze Parliament is a fundamental political right of MPs, taking precedence over established norms of democratic functioning. All else is political theatre.

The comptroller and auditor general's report on the 2G scam turns up little that was not known before. It was well known in 2008 at the time of licence allocation that Raja had subverted the process by first decreeing that licences would be given on a first-come first-served basis, and then tipping off favoured parties so that they could be first in line. When some of those licences were later sold at astronomical prices, many journalists highlighted the huge sums the government had foregone by not having an auction.

In no well-governed country are scarce licences handed out in such a manner. How on earth can a queuing system reward the most deserving? In any case, the licences were won, not by those who applied first but by those who first submitted the required documentation, and these were the ones tipped off through insider information. What did they pay for this inside information? Nobody knows, but everybody can guess.

It is easy to point fingers at Raja, but Manmohan Singh and his cabinet went along with this disgraceful licensing formula, and so are fully culpable. Even the Marxists, who are now waxing eloquent with rage, are culpable. They had the ability to topple the government in 2008 when the 2G licences were awarded, and actually tried to use this ability in regard to the Indo-US nuclear deal. But they never even tried to stop the 2G licensing formula that was obviously tailored for corruption.

Not even the BJP made a really big fuss. The truth is that all parties made so much money through dubious distributions of permits and licences in various states that they could not summon enough outrage in 2008 at the 2G money-making formula.

For the future, we need a law that prohibits the discretionary misuse of power apparent in so many allocations of land, mines, and licences of all sorts. We need a law that lays down that no government permit or licence shall be granted save on the basis of an auction, of which the full details and documentation are available to all, at least three weeks in advance. One exception will have to be made. An auction raises costs, and can mean that the winner has to charge high rates to recover his auction bid. In cases where the aim is to keep public prices low, licences can be distributed free of charge by lottery to pre-qualified candidates that will also be corruption-free. Any government allocation without such transparency should be legally null and void.

Of course, politicians will resist any such law. It will end the very lucrative games they have been up to all their lives. Yet politicians are sensitive to public outrage, and will give way when politically necessary. If this reform happens after the 2G scam, it will yield a public dividend several times the size of the scam itself.

This blog was written after the 2G scam came to light which led to the opposition parties stalling Parliament proceedings in December 2010.

India's shameful load of shit

Jug Suraiya | 19 March 2010

On the same day that the Economist magazine's Economist Intelligence Unit (EIU) predicted that the Indian economy would overtake that of China by 2018, and on the same day that the Lok Sabha witnessed a furore over Mayawati's Rs 5 crore garland made of 1,000-rupee notes, the TOI reported that of the one billion people all over the world who daily have to defecate in public because of lack of the most basic sanitary facilities, 58 per cent are Indians. Some 638 million of our fellow citizens — who according to the Constitution have the same rights as you and I do, including the right to vote, if they are of age — have no access to even the most rudimentary of lavatories and have no choice but to relieve themselves in full sight of others. Of these 69 per cent live in rural areas while 18 per cent are in cities and towns.

Apart from anything else, the scandalous state of affairs poses an extremely serious health hazard; human excreta is one of the most virulent spreaders of disease. The brutal necessity of having to perform in public what should be a private act can also be psychologically humiliating.

Commuters from Mumbai's suburbs, and in other parts of the country, routinely see hundreds of people squatting besides the train tracks to relieve themselves. Many of them are women, who often cover their heads with their saris, thus making themselves 'invisible' to onlookers through the inverse logic that if I can't see you (because my head and eyes are covered) you can't see me. Such 'invisible' women are India's open and only too visible shame.

The humiliation and degradation does not — and ought not to — attach to those who perforce must do what they have to do without the dignity of privacy. The shame is ours that over 60 years after independence from foreign rule we continue to be a society in which more than half the total population has no recourse but to relieve themselves in the open, like animals.

Instead of spending hundreds of crores on putting up statues of Ambedkar, Kanshi Ram and herself, and instead of accepting Rs 5-crore 'garland' from her worshippers — followers is too mild a word for such fawning adulation — Mayawati would do well to launch a project to provide clean and hygienic communal toilets in villages, towns and cities of UP. This is of particular social relevance in that the BSP's core constituency remain the Dalits, who were the age-old 'night-soil' carriers stigmatised by the upper castes.

Mayawati aside, political parties across the board should take up the challenge that Mother India is spared the daily dishonour of making public her private biological functions.

Indeed, Bindeshwar Pathak, who in 1974 launched the Sulabh Movement to provide inexpensive sulabh shauchalyas across the country would be the right person to spearhead such a project. Pathak pour-flush toilets can be installed for as little as 2,000 rupees. At the last count, more than a million of such toilets for homes and institutions had been installed in India. Millions more need to be made operative, and urgently.

Till we can draw a veil of privacy and dignity across the sight of Bharat Mata squatting to do her business, India will continue to broadcast a literally crap image of itself to the world and to ourselves, despite all the credit we lay claim to for our social and economic progress.

In the end it adds up, precisely, to a load of shit.

Sai Baba's one real miracle that no one can question

Rajesh Kalra | 27 April 2011

I am not a follower of Sathya Sai baba, or any baba, or Pope or any other religious man or Godman for that matter. I may be spiritual, but I am not religious. I never visit temples or churches or gurudwaras or mosques or any other religious place unless accompanying friends of that particular faith, or the place has some historical or cultural significance that interests me. So, I would visit the cathedral at Chartres or the Golden Temple at Amritsar or any temple anywhere, just for the reasons mentioned above.

I remember when I visited the holiest site of Hindu pilgrimage — Kailash-Mansarovar — a few years ago, while the sundry swamis and gurus and all others were totally overawed by the occasion, I remember getting overawed by the prospect of trekking in the region and the natural beauty alone, with zero religious overtones. It is with that background that I now begin the real reason of this post.

In the reams written about Sathya Sai baba's life and death and the millions of followers he has/had, I have honestly been unmoved. I agree with the rationalists that if he were indeed God and had supernatural powers, why would he die like a normal human being, after being supported by life-support systems for almost a month? There are then tons written about his so called powers that would conjure up material goods out of thin air and also how several rationalists call him a trickster or a fraudster who merely indulged in magical tricks to impress and win the confidence of the gullible. I agree with that too.

But just as I doubt the miracles attributed to him, I hold the same view on miracles attributed to all other saints and godmen and godwomen, of all religions. Having said that, however, I still have no hatred or ill-will towards them. On the contrary, I hold them in high esteem.

First of all, I think there has to be something that all these people possess that makes millions follow them blindly. It is something that cannot be wished away. And when you dig deeper, you see the reason and that is the reason I respect them.

The faith of the millions comes from the genuine philanthropic work that these guys undertake. In the case of Sai baba, for example, he transformed a small village into a hub of education and health facilities. He brought water to some of the most water starved areas of the state, paying for it from his trust. All this is something that the state could never have achieved by itself. A fellow cyclist in my group is now a General Manager with a top BPO firm in the country. He studied at the university set up by Sai Baba.

Like him, there would be millions who benefited from what Baba's trust set up. It is the lives of such people that he touched, millions of them through his life that treat him as God. To them, he brought about unimaginable improvement to their lives and irrespective of what rationalists like me may say, baba was a God to them.

To me, this is test enough as a citizen. We need more doers like him. Even if some brand them tricksters or fraudsters, I would rather have them benefit all segments of the society than having to grapple with crooks who masquerade as our rulers and resort to nothing but cheating.

This blog was written when Sathya Sai Baba was hospitalized and was on life-support system.

Calling Bengali/Bihari V Kuriens

TK Arun | January 13, 2011

Rising prices of vegetables and of other articles of food are a problem, of course, but also an opportunity to give a boost to the incomes of rural producers, with a little imagination and organisation.

Two states that can deliver a swift boost in farm production and productivity are Bihar and Bengal, with their fertile soil and water ever present on the surface or just below it. Assam would also qualify, except for its greater logistical challenges in getting the produce to the rest of the country.

Policy is perennially schizophrenic when it comes to farm prices. Jai Kisan, shouts the government and promptly clamps down on exports whenever food prices turn up the political heat.

Procurement prices are the same as minimum support prices, and the latter are hiked every now and then, and surprise feigned when food commodity prices go up. Except in the case of procured grain, the link between the price the consumer pays and the price received by the farmer is tenuous. Middlemen not only add on huge margins but also are in a position to inflate these margins at the slightest indication of a supply shortfall.

A supply chain and trading system that give such enormous leverage to middlemen do serious damage of two kinds: one, transmission of the price signal arising at the consumer all the way to the farmer turns fuzzy and, two, the trader acquires the power to manipulate prices. An organised retail industry is the only thing that can tackle this.

Organised retail brings Wal-Mart to mind. But why? Mother Dairy in Delhi and its counterparts around the country in the cooperative sector are also organised retail. Amul is an example of an efficient, farmer-friendly supply chain management company that captures the bulk of the price paid by the retail consumer for the farmer. We need to build more such institutions.

Opening up organised retail to foreign direct investment has been a major area of debate. The energies wasted in this would be better spent in building up a wholly domestic retail chain with the farmer as the starting point. We launched Operation Flood when resources were meagre and technology rudimentary, but Vergehese Kurien's pioneering cooperative movement built India's dairy sector into the world's largest.

Today, when the resources at our disposal are far greater and knowhow, far more sophisticated, we should be able to outdo Operation Flood. Instead, we have Paralysis Trickle.

However, Bihar and Bengal do not need to wait for a new distribution chain to be built to step up farm production and feed fast-growing India's rising appetite for food, superior foods and non-food agricultural commodities. In the short run, they can act to step up the output of vegetables of all kinds.

The increase in supply will both find ready takers in the existing retail formats, and halt the rise in vegetable prices. Since reining food prices in is of immense political significance for the Centre, it should be possible for these states to negotiate special devolution schemes from the Centre, linked to time-bound delivery of additional food output. These should be able to cover most of the outlay the state governments need to make in the effort.

What is crucially needed is organisation and administration, and money plays a secondary role. The crop that is best suited for a production boost in each micro region has to be identified fast. In all probability, the data exists, in local farm lore, if not in the regional agricultural university or some colonial catalogue meticulously compiled to make the best possible use of India's resources.

The government could make the needed inputs available, including seeds, manure, micro-nutrients and crop husbandry practices, but without subsidy.

Organising scattered, small-scale producers into production units that use standardised farming practices and seeds and other inputs and do so in coordination with one another is one crucial task. The other is procurement of the produce, its cleaning, packaging, sale, despatch and delivery to bulk consumers with speed, hygiene and efficiency while realising the best possible price and kicking it back to the producers.

What these tasks call for are new commercial organisations. Farmer companies, in which all members have the same voting rights and are free to sell stake to outside investors, should be just as welcome as cooperatives of the Amul kind. Let multiple companies/cooperatives be formed in each region.

It would be a good idea to invite fresh graduates of the IIMs and IRMA to lead these enterprises. The challenge and the opportunity to prove their worth should be sufficient incentive for young talent, even if a chance to solve the world's food crisis and step into V Kurien's shoes looks too daunting.

Enabling swift registration of companies/coops, keeping at bay the tentacles of red tape and seed capital should be the states' contribution. Enthusing small producers to embark on a new adventure should be the prime contribution of political leadership.

Buddha and Nitish have little to lose by giving this a good try, and a whole new world to win, if they succeed. Let's hope they will.

Turn Adarsh into a monument of shame

Shobhaa De | 23 January 2011

Roughly seven years ago, my two older children had to deal with a situation I wouldn't wish on my worst enemy. It involved a small army of hired goons sent by an unscrupulous builder to oust them from their ancestral home. Their aged grandmother had to face this mob by herself. They had made themselves comfortable in her living room, asked for the television set to be switched on and informed her casually that this was now their home and they were there to stay. She was a lady with remarkable reserves of fortitude and did not panic even when these strangers spread out their bedding, opened tiffin boxes and settled in for the night. I was out of the country at the time. There is just so much one can achieve through frantic telephone calls to the local police station, the municipal guys of that ward and the MLA or MP elected to represent the interests of his constituency. It was evident from the buck-passing and evasive responses I encountered that almost everyone was deep in it in one way or the other. Those desperately traumatic 48 hours of the children being bulldozed and threatened by the builder and asked to vacate or else, shall never be forgotten.

Does this story have a happy ending? Umm. Not really. Left with few options, the family had to accept a lousy settlement and move out with dignity. Too much was at stake — especially an old lady's precarious health. We were advised to fight the goons with goons, and get some influential 'higher ups' to intervene. None of that happened, mainly because the builder's reach went all the way to the top! And a vastly admired heritage property was pulled down and replaced by an entirely illegal shopping centre with escalators that open out to an overcrowded street in central Mumbai. Today, the builder is in trouble for cheating, forgery and deception. Will anything happen to the villain? No chance. Will the hideous shopping complex be demolished? Are you kidding? This is Mumbai. This is where an 'Adarsh' happens ...with absolute impunity.

This brings me to Adarsh and the current debate about demolishing the notorious structure. Pretty pointless, don't you think? Demolish it just to show the world 'action is being taken'? And then what? If Adarsh does indeed come crashing down within seconds, using the implosion technique (wow! Aren't we impressed?), what purpose will it serve other than to create headlines and get our spiffily dressed minister for environment and forests to preen some more on camera and pat himself on the back for showing everybody he means business? Frankly, I don't see the demolition happening. Not in the near future, perhaps never. There are at least five buildings in the same area that are disputed structures. These have been around for decades — ghostly and abandoned, with no decision in sight. Like Adarsh, Mumbai has a Pratibha too — another high profile residential tower that became the focus of a nasty battle. Pratibha is still there — we have stopped bothering about what will happen to it. Just as we'll forget Adarsh after a couple of months. That's how it goes. Adarsh is considered 'hot' by the media. It may lose its 'hotness' quotient if a bigger scam comes up. And, as has been pointed out by various legal luminaries, where does this Adarsh imbroglio end and another begin? There are hundreds of similar scandals in Mumbai alone. Each time one turns around to gasp at yet another spectacular construction selling at an astronomical price, the unanswered questions remain the same — who cleared the project? For how much? If one were to probe a little, nearly every new high rise has irregularities galore — serious lapses that can endanger the lives of occupants. But who bothers with paperwork that has no meaning in the first place? Whose signatures are on those files? Surprise! Signatures of the very same bureaucrats responsible for okaying Adarsh. If today a Lt Col R K Singh is asking why he, legitimate owner of a flat in Adarsh, is being penalized for the wrongdoings of others, what response can he expect? This person is paying rent, plus repaying EMIs on the loan he'd taken to buy that precious flat. Can he demand compensation – and if so, from whom? If Jairam Ramesh has his way, Singh's dream home could soon be rubble. Singh had fought the Kargil war in the Drass sector and paid a substantial amount to acquire the flat. As did Commander Rajiv Pilo, who was part of the naval force at Kochi during the 1971 war. His savings are invested in an Adarsh flat. Will he get his money back?

It would appear there are no honest builders left in Mumbai. The food chain in this highly lucrative business is very inclusive – and everybody 'eats money' – from the lowly clerk to the mighty neta. Land is getting snapped up faster than lingerie at a Victoria's Secret sale. The shadowy promoters are known to all, but everybody feigns instant amnesia. And God help us, but the CBI has been entrusted with cracking the Adarsh case and we know its dismal success rate only too well. If the CBI sleuths are still searching for Aarushi's killer, do we really expect them to nail those behind the Adarsh scandal ? Dream on!

Adarsh should stay. There is rich irony in both its name and continued existence. Let Adarsh be converted into a Museum of Corrupt Practices. It could become a tourist attraction like the Leaning Tower of Pisa. A towering monument that commemorates national shame. Who knows, it may even make its money back through ticket sales to the venal babus who built it.

Badhiya hai!

A sense of deja vu

Pritish Nandy | 15 May 2011

One of the problems of being around on this planet for a while is that one begins to see most things in a slightly skewed perspective. You look back in time to context current events. The successes others around you are constantly exulting in do not impress you that much simply because you know tomorrow always comes, whether Garth Brooks wants it or not. No, it doesn't mean one is a cynic or a disparager. It only means one learns from history. If we don't, as the wit said, we are condemned to repeat our mistakes.

Like most Bengalis I am elated Mamata Banerjee has won. She is a gutsy person and has built her organisation from scratch to take on the mighty Left citadel which she brought crashing down last friday. The media which abandoned its neutrality in politics a long time back celebrated her victory with as much delight as her Trinamool workers playing Holi on the streets. I may be however forgiven for feeling a bit disappointed that journalists, unlike in my time, have abjured their impartial roles and become as much a part of politics as party workers. Newspapers, magazines, news channels today side with political parties at election time making it difficult for common people to separate facts from propaganda, truth from disinformation. I hated the media's original rejection of Mamata and bootlicking of the Left as much as I dislike their new found love for her and hatred of the Left.

The media's job is to inform. It is up to you and me to assess that information and decide who we want to support. Mamata with her easy, street smart charm could have easily won this battle on her own. Just as Gautam Deb would have easily lost the battle for the Left by his aggressive, uncouth posturing. The media needed to referee the confrontation instead of conjoining it. But that's another matter. I am happy Mamata won and gave the Left a rest after 34 years of running West Bengal, largely into the ground. But the funny thing is: I recall when the Left Government came to power and Jyoti Basu became chief minister, he said exactly the same things Mamata is saying today and we applauded him exactly as we are applauding Mamata now. People flowed out onto the streets to celebrate the victory of the red revolution. Just as they are doing today, to celebrate Trinamool's green revolution.

Tamil Nadu is the same. I hear Jayalalitha saying the same things today, to thunderous applause, that I heard Karunanidhi say when she was chucked out by the electorate and the DMK came in with so much hope and fanfare. The first thing Jayalalitha said on Friday after her landslide victory was: The people of Tamil Nadu have voted out corruption. Those were the exact first words of Karunanidhi when he defeated her last time. She was then seen as the symbol of corruption. Many bribery cases were filed against her. Today, she admonishes the DMK with precisely the same words and the electorate loves it. It's not only because of our collective amnesia. It's also because a new generation of voters comes out in every election with no memory of the past. It's charming to see their gullibility and hope, their dreams of change.

Actually our choices are very limited in most polls. We are forced to decide between really awful people. The "none of the above" button which voters have been demanding for ages has still not been given presumably because there's a fear that most voters will actually press it. As a result, a consortium of crooks, rascals and fixers run our polity with shameless disregard for issues of morality and public trust. Luckily, the nation has finally woken up to the fact that it's possible to resist them, punish them, put them behind bars with a little bit of help from institutions like the Supreme Court which still function with their head held high in an environment where most crawl on all fours and seek favours from the corrupt. No wonder there's so much of anger and angst all around.

Elections give people a chance to vent their ire, to show their power. To prove that our democracy still flourishes despite so many disappointments and disconnects. Mamata's victory, the DMK's abject defeat, the Left losing both Kerala and West Bengal, Gogoi's third term, the Karnataka by-elections: all these are signs that India is doing well. We know how to use the ballot to win back the freedoms we occasionally misplace. But, yes, we also need to remember our past so that we make the right choices. We need to learn the lessons history teaches us. That's the only way we can look ahead with courage and faith instead of wallowing in self pity, flagellating ourselves for our many failures. If we make mistakes, as indeed we often do, we know that we can always right them at the next polls.

Is it time to acknowledge the Gujarat 'miracle'?

Swapan Dasgupta | 16 January 2011

It is a commentary on the bizarre priorities of our information order that investment commitments totalling $450 billion, equalling nearly one-third of India's GDP, are either ignored or put on par with anodyne political statements. This, however, is not the occasion to lament the lack of even-handedness in the treatment of anything remotely connected to Gujarat chief minister Narendra Modi. It is the time to celebrate something that is fast becoming undeniable: the emergence of Gujarat as the economic powerhouse of India.

Last week, there was a stark contrast between a Gujarat bubbling with optimism and the rest of the country despairing over economic mismanagement and missed opportunities. It is not that all the MoUs signed at the fifth Vibrant Gujarat summit will be translated into reality. Many will remain paper commitments. But when the who's who of Indian industry line up to proclaim their faith in Gujarat as a wholesome place for investment, having already put their money where their mouth is, neither India nor the rest of the world can afford to be in denial.

The proclamations of faith in Gujarat are all the more meaningful because they have been made despite the Centre's unremitting displeasure with anything that could bolster Modi's credentials. Modi doesn't usually win awards for being the "Reformer of the Year" or for innovative governance. In fact, he doesn't even make it to the shortlist. But he has invariably secured an unequivocal thumbs-up from those who have a real stake in the emergence of India as a world economic power.

The skeptics, who insist that the rise and rise of Gujarat has little to do with the state government, are partially right. Entrepreneurship and business are part of the Gujarati DNA, a reason why Mukesh Ambani stated that Reliance Industries has always proudly cloaked itself in the Gujarati business ethos. But Gujaratis have been under no obligation to sink their money into Gujarat: from Dholera to Durban, the world has been their karmabhoomi.

The reason Gujarat has registered the highest, double-digit GDP growth in the past decade owes much to the targeted, business-friendly approach of its government. Four features stand out. The first is quick decision-making — what Modi has dubbed the "red carpet, not red tape" approach. Ratan Tata, for example, recounted how the land allotment for the Nano project was completed in just three days, a quick-fire decision that has fetched Gujarat some Rs 30,000 crore in Tata group investments and direct employment for some 50,000 people.

The second feature is the curious phenomenon of the near-absence of political corruption at the top. Even Modi's worst enemies will not deny that the chief minister's fanatical personal integrity has had a salutary trickle-down effect. Irritated by politically inspired extortion, industry has identified Gujarat as a place where it is possible to do ethical business.

Third, Gujarat since 2002 has been marked by social peace. Particularly important for industry is the absence of rural unrest, which unseated Tata Motors from West Bengal and is now so marked in Maharashtra and Karnataka. This is because Gujarat has bucked a national trend and is witnessing high growth in agriculture — last year the sector grew by 9.9%. This means that farmers now have a stake in the larger prosperity of the state and aren't swayed by populists and Maoists.

Finally, the growth of Gujarat has been spurred by a philosophy of "minimum government and maximum governance". In plain language, this means that the state government has concentrated on creating the infrastructure for growth and left it to the private sector to get on with the job of actual wealth creation. In Gujarat, politicians don't talk the language of class conflict; they too mirror the preoccupation with *dhanda* (business). So all-pervasive is the respect for enterprise that even the children's amusement park in Ahmedabad has created kiddie games centred on the use of virtual money!

The extent to which this vibrant Gujarati capitalism will benefit Modi's national ambitions is difficult to predict. But one thing is certain. As Gujarat shines and acquires an economic momentum of its own, more and more businesses will find it worthwhile to channel a major chunk of their new investments into Gujarat. The Centre may not like the resulting uneven growth but the alternative is not to thwart Gujarat by political subterfuge — such as preventing public sector banks from engaging with the state government and the whimsical use of environmental regulations. Gujarat has shown that accelerated and sustained growth is possible when the state plays the role of an honest facilitator, rather than a controller.

Modi didn't create the Gujarati character; he was moulded by it. He merely gave it a contemporary thrust and an ethical dimension. If politicians focused on these, India will be a much better place.

What makes Kashmiri youth angry

Rajesh Kalra | 09 March 2011

I was invited earlier this week for a closed-door session on Kashmir. Almost everyone at the session, except me, was someone who has a direct role to play in the state and its growth, be it administration – civil and defence – policy makers, thinkers or prominent residents. Honestly, the immediate reaction at seeing the gathering and also the seriousness with which they were discussing an important issue made one feel good. This was neither an official meeting, nor was it a Track II initiative. It was, at best an academic exercise but the honchos sat through patiently, nevertheless.

While I am not at a liberty to disclose the exact contents of the deliberations, what was clear is that despite all the good intentions, we may actually be missing the wood for the trees. There was much discussion on what is wrong and what can be done in terms of security scenario and other things, but what was completely missing was that everyone seemed to forget the human angle to this entire issue.

I had an interaction with almost 200 students from two big universities of Kashmir a couple of months ago. The bright kids, that included girl students as well, spent almost two days in Delhi meeting people from all walks of life and explaining to them what problems they face. To me, any solution of the problem should start with interacting with these youngsters. Let me share what came across during my interactions with them.

Almost every youngster I engaged with had a deep-rooted suspicion of India. And it needed just a bit of goading to understand why. They genuinely believe that the central government and the local administration are not interested in their well-being. This perception is, in fact, so strong, that they were uniformly seething with rage against "India". And it is this perception that the administration has completely failed to address. This results in these impressionable kids believing everything against the Indian state. It needs very little effort for the mischief makers to feed them any nonsense, convincingly. It could be anti-India lies about the killing of innocents, or who was behind the killings or even the hugely exaggerated numbers that are bandied about to show as if some sort of a genocide is taking place, whereas in reality it may not even be a fraction of that. In such surcharged atmosphere, almost anything is lapped up.

Why is it that these kids, who seemed so normal to me in their behaviour with me one on one, turned so rabid when they spoke as a group? A little more scratching the surface and a lot more tumbled out. It is almost the same story that one notices in the rest of the country — the non-inclusive growth. Every kid felt that the great India growth story has passed them by. They know how the world sees India. They have seen the success stories in areas where they genuinely feel they could have done well if provided a chance, BPO sector, for one.

Also, they were all aware of how huge sums of money were being sent by Delhi for development in the state, but barely a fraction, if at all, reached them. They have seen big politicians, and even officers from the central government, turn into fat cats pocketing money that was meant for their welfare. This happens all over, one may argue. Sure, but then, there is no Pakistan and its nefarious interests working on kids in all other states as they are in Kashmir.

Speaking to the kids, it was clear the way we look at them needs to change. They need to be handled with the sensitivity that the current administration, both at Centre and in the state have shown either a disinclination for or are incapable of addressing. Our approach has always been to react to developments and situations. There is barely any proactive approach, and if at all such an attempt is made, it is riddled with corruption and inept implementation that does more harm than good. Also, we seem to live in a fool's paradise. For example, almost anybody with an ear to the ground knew as far back as in the winter of 2009 that something big is brewing in the state and had shared these inputs with authorities. But to no avail and the stone-pelting mobs' protest showed how the administration was totally ill-equipped and unprepared to tackle them. By all accounts, things are simmering under the surface even now.

One is not saying the security angles should be ignored or downplayed, if anything, they need to be strengthened, but that has to go hand in hand with improved intelligence and even more importantly, a genuine people-to-people contact is required to win over the people of the state, especially the youngsters.

I am more than convinced that handled well, they will be an asset to our nation. It will be good if we can give them the confidence that the government is serious about their welfare. That there will be opportunities available for their growth. That the money that is meant for development will be used for that purpose alone. More importantly, the results should be visible on ground. Also, we must desist from serving them platitudes, for it will most certainly backfire. I have seen their reactions to platitudes and it certainly won't work.

Apart from all this, we have to stop branding them anti-India, pro-Pak, etc. I can tell you most of them are not. They are just impressionable kids who feel let down by their own government and think they would have been better off on their own and are justifiably angry. They need to be handled with tact. Once we have handled this part well, which is a tall order, the perception change that we so desperately want, would be far easier than anyone thinks it is. A tough task no doubt, but achievable with commitment.

Tackling Maoism: lessons from Andhra

SA Aiyar | 21 March 2010

In the 1990s, only 15 of India's 630 districts suffered from Maoist incidents, but today over 200 districts are affected. Despite big increases in anti-terrorism outlays, Maoists have become much stronger in most states. The big exception is Andhra Pradesh, where Maoist incidents fell from 576 in 2005 to 62 in 2009, Maoist killings from 211 to 17, and police deaths from 25 to zero.

Andhra Pradesh has had a specialized anti-Maoist force, Greyhounds, since the 1980s. But for decades politicians avoided cracking down: they opted for peace talks with the Maoists, which the latter used to regroup and re-arm. In the 1990s the Maoists expanded stridently, controlling large areas in the northern districts and Srisailam forest belt. The houses and relatives of MLAs were attacked with impunity, and in some places, none dared campaign during elections.

What has changed in the last five years? State economic advisor Somayajulu claims that economic development and welfare have transformed the situation. Massive irrigation, construction and welfare programmes have created so much employment and income that Maoism has lost its attraction for once-unemployed youths. The casual labour wage in the state is now well above the minimum wage of Rs 120 per day, which itself has doubled in five years. Welfare schemes, notably rice at Rs 2 per kilo, have provided safety nets. So, says Somayajulu, economic progress and welfare have spearheaded the state's success against Maoism.

Chief Minister Rosiah disagrees. Yes, higher wages and employment have helped, he says, but purposive police action has been the key. He fears that a newly created Telangana state will have smaller police and economic resources and lack the strength to combat the Maoists, who have taken refuge across the state border in Chhattisgarh.

Top police officers offer several reasons for their success. First, an additional 37,000 police posts were sanctioned, though these have only partially been filled. Second, much better training gave the state's police training academy a reputation for quality.

Third, a dense network of roads, police stations, schools and sundry government offices were created in the northern forest belt adjoining Chhattisgarh. Public works created jobs and ration shops offered cheap rice. The Maoists had earlier occupied areas virtually vacated by the state. The state now reoccupied these areas.

New technology greatly helped improve police communications. The police could now intercept messages between Maoists. Modern arms and additional jeeps, motorcycles and trucks, operating on newly created road networks, gave the police unprecedented mobility and ability to find and attack Maoists.

Often, if a Maoist leader was captured or killed, the rest of the cadre collapsed. Maoism was not based on strong grassroots support. Rehabilitation schemes were announced and implemented for Maoists who surrendered, and public works created new jobs.

Additional police stations alone could not have done the trick. What worked was the proliferation of all government offices and welfare services, showing that the functionaries of the state would now stay and not leave space open for Maoists. Locals could see a new political will to battle Maoism, not strike bogus peace deals as in the past. This enabled the police to create an intelligence network based on very local knowledge, and this network was able to penetrate the Maoist cadres. That was the turning point.

The lessons for other Maoist-affected states are clear. They need stronger, modernized police forces and intelligence that can penetrate Maoist groups. They require dense road networks and the creation of a full range of government offices and services in the affected areas.

But Chhattisgarh lacks resources for this. Besides, Raipur is very distant from the Bastar forests where AP's Maoists have now taken refuge. The area has very few roads or government offices. The state is not visible, and Maoists thwart its entry.

The solution surely is a joint project of Andhra Pradesh and Chhattisgarh. It will be easier to move north from Andhra Pradesh than move south from Raipur to tackle Maoism: to build roads, government offices and police stations, and undertake public works and welfare schemes. Mere police coordination between the states will not suffice. They need to collaborate in all state functions. Chhattisgarh will need to subcontract some important functions to Andhra Pradesh, instead of just subcontracting law and order to Salwa Judum vigilantes.

This will need massive central funding and political oversight from New Delhi. Andhra Pradesh knows that driving Maoists into Chhattisgarh is not a permanent solution: they will come back. They need to be tackled in their sanctuary in Chhattisgarh, not just by police force but also by providing the full range of government services and welfare. Such cross-border provision will be difficult and complex, but is imperative.

No cricket diplomacy, please

Robin David | 29 March 2011

Frankly, as a die-hard cricket fan, I feel we could have done without heavy-duty India-Pakistan politics during the World Cup semi-final at Mohali. If Manmohan Singh and Yousuf Raza Gilani wanted to talk peace, they could have done so in a zillion cosy places in Delhi, far away from Mohali. The fact that India will take on Pakistan for a place in the final of the most prestigious cricket tournament was heavy-duty enough for me.

As if the pressure of the game was not enough, we have now added the pressure of history and politics on both teams.

But all that apart, in the presence of prime ministers and bureaucrats, the players will have to be on their best behaviour. That, I feel, will take away some of the passion from the game. When you are talking about peace and building bridges between two acrimonious neighbours, you can't expect the cricketers to display bad blood on the field. All symbolic gestures would have no meaning if peace does not prevail on the field.

In effect you can't expect the Javed Miandad-like frog-leap from any of the Pakistani players if MS Dhoni gives them an earful or Gautam Gambhir facing off against Shahid Afridi with an (un) healthy exchange of expletives during the semi-final.

I would any day enjoy a show of emotion on field rather than giving the two teams members certificates in good behaviour. The few instances of acrimony in the past have become folklore with the fans. Would Aamir Sohail have dared to tell Venkatesh Prasad to go fetch the ball after hitting him for a four in the quarterfinals of the 1996 World Cup at Bangalore if the prime ministers of India and Pakistan were in the stadium? I doubt it. That would have robbed all cricket fans a chance to witness that great reply that Prasad finally gave Sohail by sending his stumps flying and showing him the way to the dressing room.

Most fans have turned the clock back and watched that charged-up moment in cricket history at least once on YouTube.

Although, one can still expect the odd expletive exchange during the semi-final, I fear we are mostly going to see players giving each other brotherly pats and watered-down smiles after bumping into each other. Not because they really love each other, but because the two countries are in confidence-building mode. after the 26/11 attacks.

So, don't expect Gambhir to give it back to Afridi, like he did during the third one-day international at Kanpur in the 2007 series. Afridi had initiated the face-off and was fined 95% of his match fee while Gambhir lost 65% for "conduct unbecoming and bringing disrepute to the game".

Yes, I know this is a gentleman's game, but I would not mind some play of passion as well. There is just too much at stake for both teams and asking the players to behave like disciplined schoolboys is unfair.

The verbal fireworks give new meaning and an edge to the cricketing history between the two countries. Besides, I can't imagine Prime Minister Singh leaning over and asking Gilani to extradite Hafiz Saeed and Zaki ur Rehman Lakhvi to India for the 26/11 attacks, while fans are shouting themselves hoarse during the match. So what's the point...

This blog was written before India took on Pakistan in a semi-final clash in the Cricket World Cup 2011 to be played in Mohali, Punjab.

What PM should learn from Dhoni

Shobhaa De | 17 April 2011

My andawala, Raeesmiya, is a bent old man in his 70s with a serious heart condition. He is originally from Lucknow. Yes, he confesses tiredly, he's a long way from home and longs to retire there some day. But he says, with a philosophical shrug, he can't think of it, not at this stage of his life. Why can't he? His two sons are doing well; his grandchildren are healthy and happy; his wife is willing to look after him in the autumn of his life. What's his excuse? He leans forward, looks over his shoulder surreptitiously and whispers, *Bhrashtachaar!* I can't handle it any more. Mumbai has its corruption.

But Lucknow! *Hadh ho gayi.* He seems resigned to the thought of spending the remaining years of his life cycling from building to building, delivering bread and eggs to his regular customers. Over the years, I have seen the bright gleam in his eyes reduced to a sad flicker when he says, *Purana zamana hi theek tha.* By that he means life under the British! I wasn't sure I'd heard right the first time he said that. So, he repeated it a few more times. And we left it at that. It's a pretty damn depressing comment for any citizen of India to be making 63 years on. But there it is.

I met Raeesmiya the morning after our historic World Cup victory and asked him if he'd watched the match on TV. Indeed he had... his eyes were shining again. Just like old times. What did he think of the match? Dhoni? The team? He shut his eyes and exclaimed, "If only Manmohan saab could learn from these jawan boys! Just look at how they have enhanced our *desh ki shaan. Wah! Allah ki dua*!. After a brief, euphoric chat, he picked up his heavy basket and left. His eyes were still shining. Well... countless eyes were shining for at least a week after Dhoni lifted the magnificent Cup, along with the spirits of a disillusioned and angry nation.

Comparisons and conclusions between Prime Minister Manmohan Singh and our cricket captain were inevitable. It was all about effective leadership and leading from the front. Something poor Manmohan Singh has never been able to do (his hands and feet being tied). Sachin (the Legend of Legends) called Dhoni the best captain he'd played under. That is a huge compliment coming from the Master Blaster. In the political context, can Pranab Babu say that in all honesty about our PM? And, err... who will carry Manmohan Singh on their shoulders around the stadium called India? Over a billion people will happily do that for Anna Hazare, though!

One wonders what Manmohan Singh's takeaway was from the final game against worthy opponents, Sri Lanka. Surely he must have noticed a few of the bold, unconventional, individualistic and risky decisions taken by Dhoni (changing the batting order being just one of them)? And surely, he must have applauded the manner in which the entire team played as a tightly knit, well-oiled winning machine, supporting each other's strengths, covering up weaknesses, all the way?

How did Dhoni do it? Not by waving a magic wand. Not through bulldozing and badgering. And certainly not by looking the other way when his boys were tripping up or losing heart. Everybody agrees only Dhoni could have pulled it off, and as convincingly too because Dhoni has shown over and over again that he plays with a straight bat. Simple. And expects the same from his team. Dhoni also doesn't play favourites and treats every player with the same respect. Dhoni is smart enough to realize he doesn't have all the answers and seeks the guidance of seniors, even juniors, besides listening attentively to the team manager. Dhoni audaciously puts himself on the line when he has to (Sreesanth!) and takes his chances when he needs to (making Sachin bowl). He's a man who knows his mind and speaks it (no mincing words, not even about his earlier lacklustre performances). He has transformed what was considered a good team into a world class one through strategic planning and total commitment.

This spectacular win was no fluke. The first people to admit as much are his critics and they do so ungrudgingly. There is much to learn from Dhoni. And if Manmohan Singh keeps his eyes, ears and heart open, it's still not too late to start reversing the damage done to a bruised nation. A leader who's good at his job instinctively realizes when to push ahead and when to back off. A leader also knows whom to give credit to... in Dhoni's case, that one person was clearly Sachin, but he made sure all the other key players in India's win (Gautam, Virat, Zaheer and of course, Yuvraj) were duly acknowledged, as was every player in the team. Dhoni demonstrated admirable restraint (that's one powerful trait he shares with the prime minister) all through the dramatic season. Perhaps, that's the key common attribute that Manmohan Singh should capitalize on and adopt — Dhoni's Mr Cool attitude. No matter what the provocation. Tough, but achievable.

Team India has shown the world what it's capable of on the cricket field. It's high time the other Team India scores a similar victory in the global arena. Come on, Manmohan Singh — go for it! If all else fails, induct Dhoni into your cabinet! For all our sakes.

An encounter with Niira Radia

Kingshuk Nag | 22 November 2010

There was a certain mystique around Niira Radia when I met her. It was possibly in 2003 and I was in Ahmedabad as resident editor of The Times of India. A common friend said that she had expressed a desire to meet me. I was not unwilling to touch base with her, given the reputation she had already built.

The daughter of a Sharma family in East Africa — her father was apparently an agent for GE aircraft engines there — young Niira took a fascination for the aircraft and airlines business. Eventually Niira got married to an overseas Gujarati from Porbunder, who was also based somewhere in East Africa. Her interest in airlines took her close to Singapore International Airlines (SIA), which at the turn of the century was trying to enter the Indian aviation sector in partnership with the Tatas. That afforded her an introduction to Ratan Tata.

The senior industrialist was so impressed by the abilities of Niira that at one stroke he disbanded the in-house public relations machinery of all Tata group companies and handed over the job to Vaishnavi, a company that Niira had floated. This was the reason for my curiosity about her. Who is this lady who can persuade the mighty Ratan Tata to take such a step in the Tata bureaucratic empire? I wondered. My interest was also triggered by what an important functionary in the BJP's national office had told me. A man of unimpeachable integrity, this friend expressed surprise that a well-known holy man (not much seen in public and with a high image) had called him with an introduction to Niira.

The next time I came to Delhi, a meeting was organised at her South Extension office by the common friend. It must have been around 4.30pm when I met her. The business suit-clad Niira was quite cordial and came across as a smart, sweet-talking lady, maybe a year or two more than 40. After making some small talk (including how she used to go to the kitchen in her Gujarati in-laws' household with *ghunghat* and how she had learnt to make *rotlas*) Niira came to her purpose. But the subject was indirectly broached. "You guys have made life hell for Narendra Modi. Why can't you be more understanding of him and his policies?" she said. I asked whether along with Ratan Tata, Mr Modi had also joined her client list. She said no, only as a Gujarati *bahu* she "felt a responsibility towards the state". I told her that our coverage about the Gujarat government was based on facts and that I didn't see how we could dilute this. Anyway, Mr Modi was in touch with me and had been so even during the height of the Gujarat riots of 2002 and therefore was well in a position to communicate his "concerns" with me directly (and in fact he did this often). The meeting ended on a pleasant note, but I realised that the lady was determined to persist in her own friendly way.

A few months later, Mr Modi organised a "Vibrant Gujarat" show in Ahmedabad. It was a programme designed to attract business to Gujarat. But at that time, I guess by this time it was 2004, Narendrabhai's image has taken such a dip that many industrialists were not even willing to come to a state so business friendly as Gujarat much less share a common platform with him. One of the leading lights, who was critical of Modi's policies, was none other than Ratan Tata. So it was a surprise of surprises when Mr Tata came to the Vibrant Gujarat show, escorted by Niira Radia. My sources told me that Mr Tata was most uncomfortable and wondered what was he doing there.

The same afternoon I got a call from Niira. She said she would drop in to my office in the evening to say hi. She did not come but called to renew her request to go soft on Modi. In all fairness, I must also say that if there was a hint of any quid pro quo, it was not mouthed explicitly. Later my sources suggested that Mr Modi had given her no contract for engagement and had merely put her on test. Getting Ratan Tata to Ahmedabad was possibly one of the deliverables and at risk of sounding immodest I must say that "neutralizing" TOI must have been another.

Mr Modi is, however, a tough nut to crack at the best of times and not easy to please. My sources told me how on learning that Narendra Modi was flying to Goa from Ahmedabad on a particular trip with a one-hour halt at Chhatrapati Shivaji airport, Niira boarded the plane with lunch at Mumbai. I doubt whether the way to Mr Modi's heart is through his stomach, but Niira was able to crack the Gujarat chief minister a few years later courtesy Mamata Banerjee. As is well known, Ratan Tata was so miffed by the happenings in West Bengal that he decided to move his proposed Nano plant elsewhere. My hunch (and this is not confirmed information) is that Niira, being an adviser to Ratan Tata, had a clear idea about the specifications of the land that Tata Motors wanted. She also knew the kind of incentives that would make Ratan Tata plump for Gujarat for his Nano factory. All these details she possibly passed on to Narendra Modi, who was well prepared with land and incentives the moment Tata Motors pulled out of Singur. The basis for my hunch: states where Tata Motors executives went to scout for land had no idea about the type of location being sought. For instance, in Hyderabad (where I had meanwhile moved as resident editor), the government was given just a few hours' notice to ready a piece of land of huge dimensions, not very far from the airport. Naturally the government was clueless and lost the battle for Nano.

A lot of water has undoubtedly flowed under the bridge since the time that I met Niira. Obviously, she is in a different league now. It is clear — going by the Niira tapes — that her reach has expanded exponentially. But I wonder what made many of our worthy co-professionalists fall prey to Niira's allurements. I guess a primary prerequisite of not being vulnerable requires you to be ideologically very strong. Your value system has to be above board. Above all, the colleagues that you work with have to reflect the same level of morality and commitment. The internal environment of the company that you work in should also represent a similar level of professionalism.

One of the side-effects of liberalisation has been an exponential growth in the media. As a result, all manner of people have been sucked into the industry. Many are attracted by the (perceived) razzle and dazzle of the profession but for all of them career growth promises to be so fast that they lose themselves and their morality without even realising so. Clearly then, time for moral reaffirmation.

Vivekananda: My teen icon wore saffron

Anshul Chaturvedi | 08 January 2011

Long, long ago, I, too — unlikely as it may seem with the graying hair today — was once a teenaged rebel. Defiant, stubborn, questioning, a risk-taker, even reckless. Some of those traits I have, hopefully, retained. But the instigator of my transition from a seemingly inconspicuous docile schoolboy to this combative version was neither my college gang nor a rapper with an exotic name. It was a man long dead, having lived all of 39 years, speaking to me through fiery words that did not diminish in intensity with the passage of time.

I picked up Vivekananda's thoughts one day in class XIIth, and have not quite been able to put them down yet. Having the capability to live only a little of what he practiced, I cannot lay claim to being Eklavya to his Dronacharya status. Yet, when I was beginning to decipher the questions of right and wrong, moral and immoral, he summed it up for me the complexity of it all: 'Fear is the greatest sin my religion teaches'. Since then, I've tried to ensure that I did not commit the cardinal sin, whatever other errors I make.

In childhood, I learnt, as we all do, that convention and what everyone else thought mattered. Then I unlearnt it. "I will die a thousand deaths rather than lead a jelly-fish existence and yield to every requirement of this foolish world", the monk thundered through the years into my mindspace, and is it any wonder that I was often more of a nonconformist than anyone with a dozen tattoos, eyebrow piercings and purple hair colour could have been?

When I was at my most despondent, wondering whom to turn to for help, unsure of receiving it from anywhere, I recalled the man who wrote "Human help I spurn with my foot. He who has been with me through hills and dales, through deserts and forests, will be with me, I hope; if not, some heroic soul would arise some time or other, far abler than myself, and carry it out." I learnt to not despair for human help and reconcile to the fact that either He would chart out my survival or declare and end to my tenure here.

When I started out an inconsequential career in the back of beyond, I sometimes wondered what I was doing, whether it was all that I was worth. Vivekanda told me — "Do not be afraid of small beginnings, great things come afterwards. Be courageous." I learnt not to despair at small beginnings and have the courage of great things to follow them.

When I faced flak, I remembered the monk writing to his boys: 'Have faith that you are all, my brave lads, born to do great things! Let not the barks of puppies frighten you — no, not even the thunderbolts of heaven — but stand up and work!" He almost read my mind and explained in his fiery fashion: "the names of those who will wish to injure us will be legion. But is not that the surest sign of our having the truth? The more I have been opposed, the more my energy has always found expression." And I stood up and worked, irrespective of the disapproval of puppies and the heavens alike. And learnt to no longer cringe at those wishing to injure. And lived to tell the tale — so far!

When I faced slander and innuendo, my first reactions were hypersensitive. I itched to get even. Then I went back to the monk who was not spared when in the US by critics questioning his way of life there. And his response: "Tell my friends that a uniform silence is all my answer to my detractors. If I give them tit for tat, it would bring me down to a level with them. Tell them that truth will take care of itself..." I learnt to not respond and to believe that facts would take care of themselves.

When I wistfully looked at the twenties go by in 12-hour work days and struggle and little else, when I looked around and wondered why I had neither money nor fame and whether my non-conformity was worth anything, Vivekananda told me to wait. Wait, he said, "wait, money does not pay, nor name; fame does not pay, nor learning. It is love that pays; it is character that cleaves its way through adamantine walls of difficulties." I looked back at the worst points of my life, saw for myself whether I lasted through them because I kept the backbone straight or because I had clout or cash, got my answer, and told myself not to forget it thence.

When the instinct to do earth-shattering things egged me on, only to be killed with one look at my dismal bank balance, I asked him for answers, and he told me: "Was it ever in the history of the world that any great work was done by the rich? It is the heart and the brain that do it ever and not the purse." I stopped assuming that I was incapable of great work if my purse was empty.

It has now been many years of long hours and busy schedules, and sometimes one wants to simply be quiet and put thoughts into words, but time is scarce in the pursuit of the daily bread. But then one recalls the monk, even in his situation in life, writing to Sister Nivedita: "I was born for the life of a scholar — retired, quiet, poring over my books. But the mother dispenses otherwise — yet that tendency is there." And for a moment my master and me are kindred spirits, joined in a thought across a century.

And as I chart the journey of what years I have lived, and what years — who knows how many — are left, every single time I face something that makes me falter, ponder, slow down, I go back to my gurumantra, words of Vivekananda that are etched in my mind from that day when I first read them as a 17-year old: "This I have seen in life — he who is over-cautious about himself falls into dangers at every step; he who is afraid of losing honour and respect, gets only disgrace; he who is always afraid of loss, always loses..."

When Vivekananda taught that to a 17-year-old, he gave him freedom from fear, he made him the ultimate teenaged rebel. Except that, unlike the tattoos, the piercings or the punk cuts, you never outgrow this rebel instinct.

You gifted me the ability to stay in my mind forever 17. Happy birthday, Naren!

A nation of banias

Pritish Nandy | 26 February 2011

The much maligned caste system, complex and inscrutable as it may appear to us, once had deep roots in our society. The Brahmins pursued knowledge and statecraft. Kshatriyas fought and protected our honour and sense of nationhood. Banias ran business and trade. The sub castes (which ran into many hundreds) played their own roles. It all worked perfectly well till the lower castes, who got the rough end of the deal, began to protest. They refused to do the jobs assigned to them by history (many of which were demeaning) and sought a new status in the emerging India. This was but natural and ended up largely dismantling the edifice of caste. Merit became the new yardstick.

But the triumph of merit created its own problems. We see fewer people today doing what their forefathers did so amazingly well. Many have migrated to new jobs, without the skills required to back them. Others have become what can be best described as caste refugees. And, funnily, everyone wants to do the Bania's job. So, however skilled they may be at what they do, most people now want to be in business, make lots of money. So from a great nation of many castes, many skills we are slowly becoming, like the US, a country where everyone, from teachers to healers to rock stars believe that God sent them to this planet with the sole mission of making money. The scramble for lucre has become so obsessive, so obscene that the dignity of many professions has simply vanished.

Where have the great thinkers gone? The legendary healers? The great musicians, painters, philosophers, teachers, leaders of change? Everyone seems to have joined the Gold Rush today. Painters talk more about the price of their canvases than the magic of their craft.

Authors discuss sales graphs more than what they write about. Doctors spend more time arguing over their fees than the treatment. Teachers don't talk about acquiring knowledge. They talk about coaching classes to help you pass exams, find lucrative jobs. Even fortune tellers blindside you to love and tell you how you can make more money by wearing some silly gemstone.

Cricketers have long ceased to be sportsmen. They are like cattle, valued by how much they fetch at slave auctions. So you write off a Saurav or a Brian Lara simply because no one bid for them at the IPL. A politician's power is assessed not by what he does for India but by how much he stashes away in Switzerland. This country has become just another bazaar where everything's bought or sold, from spectrum to wakf property to pretty underage brides to seats in Parliament. Everyone's a Bania today. Everyone's trading. No one buys art to hang it on their walls. They stash it away in vaults. Over 50% of flats sold in Mumbai, possibly the world's most expensive real estate, are bought by investors or by politicians and Government officers to park their ill gotten cash. This ensures that prices stay at a level where actual home makers can't afford it.

There was a time when artists did their best work for fun. Jatin Das drew the living area of my Kolkata flat in stunning black and white, over one drunken night. It was the only reason why I never rented nor sold the flat for 26 years, even after leaving Kolkata. Friends like Husain, Manu Parekh, Samir Mondal, Manjit Bawa drew for my books of poems. No one asked for money. No one offered it. It was love, admiration, friendship that brought us together. I remember, years ago, buying a hundred Sunil Das drawings at the Kolkata art fair for ten bucks each. I gave them away to my friends. Souza gifted me so many drawings. I gave them away too. That's what art is for. My entire library of books came from authors, publishers and friends. None of my dogs were ever bought. They strolled into my home and stayed.

Life is not transactional. Nor is friendship, love, marriage, jobs. Poor as I was, I never did a job, any job for money. I came to Mumbai for a fraction of what I earned in Kolkata just because I wanted to be a journalist. I went to Parliament because I thought I could make a difference. I make movies because I enjoy it. At times we succeed. Often we fail. But money does not determine either. The questions asked are always: Did we have fun making it? Will it endure?

All around me today I see this bustling marketplace where everyone's transacting, I understand now why our forefathers created the caste system. For all its faults, it allowed our society to have currencies other than cash. There was knowledge, skill, wisdom. There was courage, honour, pride. There was art, craft, music, the mysterious science of healing. There were so many things that made life magical. Now there's just one currency driving us: Money. We have become a nation of Banias. Or, as the Americans would proudly say, entrepreneurs.

India Inc should look beyond BTech and MBA

Swapan Dasgupta | 24 October 2010

The Tata's' generous $50 million donation to Harvard Business School has, quite naturally, attracted considerable attention in India. This includes uncharitable suggestions that India's high-profile multinational has got its priorities all mixed up and is suffering from a colonial hangover.

The debate over the ethical validity of corporates directing their philanthropic energies abroad, particularly when Indian education could do with booster shots, is likely to continue. The India versus Harvard tussle is, however, only one emotive aspect of the public interest in private endowments. Equally relevant is the question: what are the donations for? In addressing this issue, it is best not to lump together all donations to overseas institutions.

The Tata donation to a premier business school has followed a path well-travelled. In India's prevailing value system, management education is the pinnacle of accomplishment, on a par with an IIT degree. An MBA is regarded as a passport to career advancement and that explains why business schools have mushroomed all over India. Indian society hasn't paused to ask the question British cartoonist Martin Rowson once posed to me in jest: "Why does a man selling envelopes in Swindon need a management degree?"

Rowson was guilty of caricature. Yet, there is a point to ponder: has India become obsessive about the MBA, at the cost of everything else?

This is why it may be instructive to look at the two other gifts to Harvard that were overshadowed by the fat Tata cheque: Anand

Mahindra's $10 million donation to the Harvard Humanities Centre and Narayana Murthy's $5 million to the Clay Sanskrit Library.

To the reigning philistines, these endowments were eccentric indulgences. Ever since Jawaharlal Nehru injected the promotion of "scientific temper" into the Directive Principles of the Constitution, Indian conventional wisdom has deemed the perusal of the humanities a colossal waste of time and an unaffordable luxury. For conspiratorial post-colonialists, the primacy of the liberal arts during the Raj was Macaulay's plot to create a nation of subordinate clerks. To economic planners concerned with a skilled workforce, classical studies or Indology was another diversion of resources. In the contrived science and technology versus humanities battle, the latter stood no chance.

The institutional devaluation of the humanities was reflected in the modified design of the all-important civil services examinations. From the day multiple-choice questions became the norm and the essay paper was junked, it became clear that lucidity and articulation — the ability to construct an elegant and internally consistent argument — were no longer regarded as worthwhile attributes.

The stress on applied skills was no doubt a shift away from an elitism that had earlier made the IAS and IFS a wing of the St Stephen's College alumni club. But, have we overdone the anti-elitism bit and, instead, bred a generation lacking lucidity in three languages?

The 'reform' of civil services recruitment was just the tip of the killer iceberg. Since S Nurul Hasan decided to make education the laboratory for some inspired ideological engineering, the humanities were inexplicably merged into the 'social sciences'. Instead of being an argumentative conversation involving the past and present, "scientific history" resulted in students being force-fed dollops of questionable certitudes. Literary criticism became jargon infested and infected with derision of 'dead, white males'. Classical studies were made lifeless by the official disdain for theology and religion. Indeed, had it not been for universities in Britain, Germany and the US, Indology as a discipline would have become extinct. The state of the Asiatic Society is living proof of the ease with which we destroyed institutions that others had so painstakingly built.

It is in the context of the relentless assault on the humanities that we can view Mahindra and Murthy's donations to Harvard as inspired choices. Murthy's gift will help complete and perhaps revive the monumental project sponsored by the philanthropist John Clay to publish the essential works of classical Sanskrit literature. Mahindra's endowment to his alma mater could inspire fellow industrialists to recognize a life beyond technology and business studies. Since India often takes its cue from 'phoren', the two donations may even prompt a larger realization that a function of education is the pursuit of knowledge for its own sake. Who knows, one of these days we may even be privileged to hear an HRD minister say that education isn't just about "scientific temper".

Cane and able: what a terrible idea, Sirji!

Shobhaa De | 13 June 2010

La Martiniere (Kolkata) is my husband's old school. For decades, he has remained one of its proudest ex-students. So embarrassingly proud that a few years ago in Karachi, when he discovered five ex-La Marts' 'boys' at the posh club where we were dining, he gathered them up and got them to lustily sing the school anthem. Such is the fierce loyalty factor La Martiniere used to generate in its vast network of alumni.

Till the horrific suicide of Rouvanjit Rawla, the class VIII student who hanged himself four months ago, unable to take the humiliation meted out to him by the school principal, Sunirmal Chakraborty, and other teachers. The lad's 'crime'? His classmates say he was 'naughty' and didn't do his homework on time. Those transgressions cost him his life.

Ajay Rawla, the boy's father took four months to overcome his shock and decide to do something about the dismal state of affairs in one of India's most prestigious schools — he lodged a police case. Had the media not been alerted, chances are the grief-stricken father's complaint would have remained a piece of paper in a forgotten file. As of now, investigations are on, and the principal has confessed to 'caning' the boy. How archaic is that word itself! Caning! Who canes kids in this day and age? And worse — calls it 'tradition'? Well, here's one principal who did just that, and thought it defence enough to justify his deplorable actions.

One would have thought this sadistic system of 'disciplining' children disappeared with the British and their ghastly public school rules. To acknowledge that this still goes on in our renowned schools is a pathetic comment on how stuck we are in a bizarre time warp that doesn't recognize the basic rights of children. Of course, caning happens in pathshalas across the country. That is equally despicable. The explanation is also absurd, but remember, the mindset of some village teachers has yet to switch gears.

Young Rouvanjit's profile is vastly different. He belonged to the urban elite of the City of Joy (such irony!). He represented the *babalog* of the *bhadralok* in our midst — privileged, affluent and aware. The school in question comes with impeccable credentials. And yet, one of their own was compelled to call it quits in the most awful way. Kapil Sibal made a strong pitch on behalf of children across the country on a TV channel when he said these bachchas were a symbol of tomorrow's India. Schools that believe in this form of barbaric discipline completely ignore the law (which is in place to protect our kids) and worse, destroy a child's confidence, sometimes for life. No matter what wrong was committed by Rouvanjit, the viciousness of the combined attacks on him (one report mentioned the cane broke on the child's back) were obviously enough for him to go in search of that killer rope with which he hanged himself. Surprisingly enough, no teacher from the school had thought it necessary to alert the Rawlas to their son's 'indiscipline' — it was easier to thrash the boy. Usual story — 'teach him a lesson.'

Reading the account and watching the television clips revived long-buried memories of being frequently caned myself as a schoolgirl. This was the punishment reserved for students who were considered 'rebellious' and 'disobedient'. I was both, and worse. But to be so severely punished for those 'failings' by the ogre of a school principal — a towering woman representing a Scottish mission? I often went home with swollen, angry red welts on my upper arms — welts that made me feel so ashamed, I hid them from my parents and said not a word about the frequent torture. I now realize, had I been less ashamed and more outraged, not only would my torture have stopped (perhaps at a huge cost — I'd probably have been thrown out of school for daring to protest), but other girls would have been spared this nasty woman's brutality. I chose to remain silent. Like Rouvanjit. The big difference being, he's dead. And I am alive to retell and relive those hellish minutes when I'd be summoned to the principal's office after standing on the yellow bench for hours, often without food or water. Why am I ready to share this dreadful part of my youth? Only to demonstrate the tragedy that our schools continue to perpetuate, and in an age when there ought to be a far better understanding of such sensitive issues. A child's mind and sensibility cannot be easily fathomed, less so 'controlled' by fiendish, cruel adults who imagine they are 'doing the right thing' by striking someone defenceless and often, voiceless.

No matter what principal Sunirmal Chakraborty says in his defence, no matter how sloppily the Kolkata police responds, no matter what kind of pressures are brought on Rouvanjit's family to withdraw the charges, it is important to keep up the pressure and punish those responsible for driving Rouvanjit to take his life. The era of adopting the so-called traditional 'cane and able' modus operandi to make errant kids toe the line are over, Mr Chakraborty.

Try reading "Goodbye Mr Chips". Try loving those children — especially the difficult ones — whose parents place their trust in you and your teachers. Better still, try therapy.

What an idea, Sirji!

Book-banning belongs to a bygone era

Robin David | 31 March 2011

The last time I checked the Wikipedia page 'List of books banned by governments' was in 2009 when the Gujarat government tried to ban Jaswant Singh's book 'Jinnah - India, Partition, Independence'. The high court had, of course, struck down the notification banning the book and the government never issued a fresh notification as it had promised.

At that time Wiki listed about 70-odd instances since 1914 where threatened governments had banned the written word. Two nations had banned the maximum books — Yugoslavia, which is not even a nation any more, and India — with nine instances each. While Yugoslavia enforced most of its bans in the 1960s, India had done it more recently.

Some other countries that appeared in the list were China, South Africa during the apartheid era, Nazi Germany, communist USSR and the UK mostly of the 1950s and 60s. This is not to say that these are the only counties to ban books. Almost all countries have done it at some point in history.

I revisited the Wiki page again on Wednesday after the Gujarat government banned Pulitzer prize-winning journalist Joseph Lelyveld's book 'Great Soul: Mahatma Gandhi and His Struggle with India'.

Almost two years later, Wiki has updated the list with nearly 100 failed and successful instances of banning books. The new additions are mostly historical attempts that had been missed out earlier, apart from Jaswant Singh's book. What is most fascinating is that India has now overtaken Yugoslavia with 13 instances!

For me, the banning of books conjures up images of Salman Rushdie and Taslima Nasreen battling for freedom against tyrannical and paranoid Ayatollahs. Especially when you consider that Lelyveld's book has not even been released in India! I can't understand how a book can be banned without being read first. Shouldn't you know first hand which sections are objectionable before deciding that it is not worthy of being read by Indians?

Banning books on the basis of hearsay and what some reviewers have to say shows how naive our censors are.

Besides, what does it say about us as a people? That we Indians are incapable of digesting sensitive material. That we need a government to tell us what is worth reading and what is not. That the great men of our nation should only be projected with a halo around their heads. Any alternative version of history, whether true and false, is best kept out of the hands of us Indians, because god knows how we will react.

Without reading Lelyveld's book, I can't say whether he has projected Gandhi as a bisexual and a racist or if it is an interpretation of the reviewers. What I can say is book-banning belongs to a bygone era when paranoid governments feared its peoples. A nation that takes pride about being a mature democracy should let its citizens decide what is worth reading and what is not.

If there is anything the ban will achieve, it is whetting people's voracious curiosity. Those who would otherwise not have picked up a copy of 'Great Soul: Mahatma Gandhi and His Struggle with India', will now try and get one for themselves. They will smuggle it into the country at the first given opportunity. And instead of discussing the Sensex, they will debate Gandhi's concept of brahmacharya and exactly what he had in mind while writing those letters to his body-builder supporter in South Africa, Hermann Kallenbach.

In fact, many Gujaratis will soon proclaim they have a bootlegged copy of the book. Don't forget Gujaratis have lived with prohibition all their lives. They understand bootlegging better than any other state.

This blog was written after Gujarat government banned Pulitzer prize-winning journalist Joseph Lelyveld's book 'Great Soul: Mahatma Gandhi and His Struggle with India'

Act against community crime

Nandita Sengupta | 22 April 2011

The Supreme Court's latest missive on khaps must be sweet music to the self-styled village councils. The apex court has reportedly said that District Magistrates will be held liable if they fail to rein in village councils – such as Haryana's khaps and Tamil Nadu's kattas – from acting like kangaroo courts. Khaps will be happy. What more can a bunch of men with mob-mentality want than for someone else to be punished for their crime? Further, the Court's faith in the police is touching.

Reports say that the apex court has also said that State machinery should institute criminal charges against khap members if they've harmed a couple. But khap panchayats have always said they do not issue directives to harm couples, let alone kill them. After the murder of a couple, khaps have invariably, and naturally so, distanced themselves from the two families involved. The men who have killed, mostly family members, are trotted off to jail. At best, a couple of men are sentenced for a murder an entire village kept quiet on. If a case makes it to the newspapers, the police come in only to maintain 'peace', buy silence, lament the state of affairs and certainly their helplessness.

The absurdly termed 'honour killings' are not like other murders. Murders of couples are only one end of a spectrum of crimes that communities inflict on their own. Community crime flourishes across India in a hundred different shades, all dark and scary – 'honour killings' only one extreme.

The focus cannot be on punishing a few individuals. The village must feel some pain. The focus must be on penalizing the village.

Villagers must be made 'stakeholders' in crimes committed with the sanction of all of them. Holding DMs liable isn't the issue really. The problem isn't with law enforcement alone; the problem is in the absence of an applicable law for community crime, which is what honour killings are.

Community crimes make it to the news almost every day. If one day it is a woman in Indore made to walk with burning coal in her hands to prove she is not a thief, the next day it is villagers near Delhi threatening to kidnap all the girls of an enemy village. Yesterday it was two widows killed for having an "affair". Recall the anganwadi worker who had her arms chopped off for defying child marriage. Or the visuals of the gruesome dragging of villagers tied to motorbikes. The blame of allowing the atrocities lies as much with the bystanders as with the actual culprits.

There's nothing to stop the economic and social sanctions that villagers impose either. In Haryana, a khap barred shops from selling any item, including cattle fodder, to the mother-sister duo of killed couple Manoj-Babli. Chandrapati was feted for having the guts to continue fighting for justice despite being isolated in her own village. But even after the court convicted the killers, the community continued to isolate Chandrapati. Her younger son keeps his identity hidden. The stories are dime-a-dozen. In UP's Kinanagar, near Meerut, stunned labourer-fathers of a teenage boy and girl killed with cutlasses by the girl's brothers (arrested) were tersely told by their khap not to grieve as it was 'meant to be'. Stealing of property by village councils, throwing out of entire families are fodder for full-page features in newspapers and that's it.

None of these crimes, all committed by community sanction, can be punished. At a public meeting, Brinda Karat said she visited the village threatened with the kidnap of its girls. This was in retaliation to a resident's elopement with a girl of the bully-village. The attention had the police register a case of 'thuggery'. Karat was stumped. In the Indore case, a couple of policemen were suspended. There's no closure and there's no stopping such behaviour. There's no law under which such crimes can be suitably dealt with.

To bring home how skewed our take on community crime is, take the example of Sunita Murmu. Her case throws into eerily sharp focus the strange workings of the nation's mind. Sixteen-year-old Murmu from West Bengal is among the 23 children who won the 2010 National

Bravery Awards for Children. Murmu even got a special mention.

Murmu was attacked when she was caught talking to a boy outside her community in their Santhal village. She was stripped, paraded naked and molested by her own tribesmen. She reportedly raced through fields across three or four villages, where no man or woman or official intervened to protect her; however, she was easy prey and was molested repeatedly. Some recorded the attacks and the MMS spread. NGOs spotted it, and police were pressured to step in. Murmu's bravery, we are told, lies in her daring to identify some of the attackers. And so we impose upon her a cold bravery award. And India plumbs its own sorry depths of insensitivity.

Murmu is certainly not the first child-woman to be stripped and paraded naked. Neither is she the first to have identified some of the molesters. But importantly, it's not enough to nab a few out of tens or hundreds of men and women who jeered at her, mocked her, who didn't step in to either stop the molesters or drag her to protection. Arrests are part of the deal only to appease the Other India. Molesters, attackers pooh-pooh their way out. Remorse, regret, guilt are alien sentiments.

Those who were asked to look at the possibilities of a law for 'honour killing' believe too that the community must face some penalty. They are thus mooting for a community crime law that brings into its ambit a range of such attacks. The idea is that the law must focus on protecting an individual's right and penalize those individuals and community organisations such as khaps who obstruct the exercise of that right. At the most basic level, that includes a person's freedom to speak to or marry of their choice. Such a law will also strengthen the voices within the community that do want to speak out but remain muted in the absence of any form of support. Into any such law must also be woven some form of sanctions on the villagers/ the community: stop funds perhaps.

In Murmu's case, what will stop her community from repeating such an attack on another 15-year-old? In twisted logic, the village might celebrate the chances of winning another bravery award. Surely, awarding punishment on the villages that have so cruelly forced a 'past' into young Murmu's life would have served the child, and the nation, better. If only there were a law to punish her tormentors. To that end, the Supreme Court's attempt at tackling the so-called 'honour killings' via DMs is more an exercise in arm wringing.

Jugaad is our most precious resource

SA Aiyar | 15 August 2010

People ask me, what exactly is *jugaad*? Global management experts attribute India's rapid economic growth to *jugaad*. In a recent survey by the Legatum Institute, 81% of Indian businessmen said *jugaad* was the key reason for their success.

Many years ago, innovative Punjabis mounted a diesel irrigation pump on a steel frame with wheels, creating a vehicle they called *jugaad*. It was ultra-cheap but did not conform to vehicular regulations. Over time, *jugaad* came to mean grassroots innovation to overcome any constraint.

In the West, innovation is done by scientists using expensive equipment. In India, it's done by every housewife, farmer, transporter, trader and industrialist. It does not require high-spending R&D: it simply needs creativity and imagination. Anil Ambani once said Reliance succeeded through innovation, not invention.

One avatar of *jugaad* is what management gurus call "frugal engineering", exemplified in the Tata Nano, the cheapest car in the world. India's telecom companies provide calls at Re 1 a minute, the cheapest in the world. Narayana Hrudayalaya and Shankara Nethralaya provide the cheapest heart and eye treatment in the world. Indian reverse-engineering of patented drugs is also frugal engineering.

Some management experts warn that *jugaad* uses any means, legal or illegal, to get a job done. They say bribery and manipulation must not be confused with genuine creativity.

I disagree. The creativity in unethical activity is, with rare exceptions, not fundamentally different from the creativity that yields frugal engineering. The incentives and rewards of the political-economic system determine whether creativity is used mainly for unethical profit or heroic productivity.

The hawala market, for instance, is used by drug lords for money laundering. But it is also an example of *jugaad*, enabling poor migrants to remit money across countries, faster and more cheaply than any formal bank system. Hawala was legal for centuries before modern governments declared it illegal.

Dhirubhai Ambani was the master of *jugaad*. The licence-permit raj made it impossible for him to progress legally, so he exploited the corruption and cynicism of the system.

He exported junk to get profitable import entitlements. He created industrial capacities vastly in excess of licensed capacity. He imported huge textile machines as "spare parts". He engineered highly profitable changes in rules for polyester imports and telecom licences. The *jugaad* he used to overcome hurdles was not distinguishable from crony capitalism.

Yet when the licence-permit raj gave way to a more open and deregulated economy, Dhirubhai used the same *jugaad* to scale dizzying heights of productivity and become world class. His giant refinery complex in Jamnagar had the highest refining margins in the world, beating the Singapore refineries. He converted to reality his vision of making telephone calls cheaper than a postcard.

Dhirubhai showed that manipulation and world class productivity are two sides of the same coin called *jugaad*. If governments create business constraints through controls and high taxes, *jugaad* will be used to overcome those hurdles. But if deregulation abolishes these hurdles, the main business constraints become lack of quality and affordability, so *jugaad* shifts to improving productivity, quality and affordability. That ultimately makes you world class.

Jugaad is amoral. If laws are oppressive, *jugaad* will seek ways round the law. Yet this amorality kept Indian business alive in the 1970s when controls were buttressed with income tax of 97.75% and wealth tax of 3.5%. Honest businessmen would have been taxed into bankruptcy. But *jugaad*, including innovative tax dishonesty, kept Indian business alive, and enabled it to surge when economic policy moved away from insane socialism.

Socialist politicians viewed themselves as golden-hearted geniuses who knew better than greedy Marwaris about what should be produced. Nobel Laureate Friedrich von Hayek pithily called this "the fatal conceit".

India may not have ample natural resources like oil or copper. But it has *jugaad*, which is more valuable. Natural resources like oil are often a curse: they can lead to government kleptocracy and authoritarianism. But *jugaad* helps foil government kleptocracy and authoritarian regulations.

Socialist planning was supposed to optimize use of India's resources. But it assigned no value at all to the marvelous innovativeness and enterprise of Indians in every branch of activity. Five-year plans sought to optimize financial resources, mineral resources (like coal and oil) and administrative resources. But they sought to crush enterprise and *jugaad*, the most precious resource of all. That has now been liberated by economic reform, and the value of *jugaad* has gained worldwide recognition.

The delivery of government services — education, health, infrastructure — remains terrible. Here too socialist control needs to be replaced by *jugaad*. Alas, politicians and socialist ideologues will not allow it.

Please don't be silent, Prime Minister

Gurcharan Das | 02 January 2011

"The things we admire in men, kindness and generosity, openness, honesty, understanding and feeling, are the concomitants of failure in our system. And those traits we detest, sharpness, greed, acquisitiveness, meanness, egotism and selfinterest, are the traits of success. And while men admire the quality of the first, they love the produce of the second." In these famous lines, John Steinbeck goes to the root of our present crisis in public morality.

He has also expressed the dilemma of every Indian mother who has to give a name to her son. Unlike the West, where everyone is called Tom, Dick or Harry, parents in India spend months trying to decide their child's name – they are, after all, forecasting its future. Torn between names that suggest goodness and success, they prudently choose success, which explains why every fifth Indian boy is called Arjun, and no one Yudhishthira.

Mahabharata's heroes come to mind because there are parallels between the epic's lament and the things we might say about our leaders today. Our republic has been in a state of continuing crises for months; the epic is a continuing repository of crises in public morality. Just as we have a problem with our governance institutions, so did the epic. What is at stake, both then and now, is our conception of success. Andimuthu Raja, former minister of telecommunications, causes us discomfort because he has undermined this conception. Until recently, Raja was a huge success in the world's eyes – he had power, money and status. Then he fell. We turn to Yudhishthira, the epic's unhero, to find out if there's another way of engaging with the world. He (and Steinbeck) raise thorny questions: What price are we willing to pay for worldly success? Is it possible to be both successful and good? Why high status cannot be conferred on a person who is honest and kind?

The problem of silence is at the heart of today's political crisis. The rage of the Indian public is over an honest Prime Minister who seems to be presiding over one of the most corrupt governments in recent Indian history. In these dark days, people have desperately wanted to clutch on to an honest man. They found one in selfless, ethical Manmohan Singh. So was Bhishma, yet he remained silent when Draupadi was being disrobed. When Draupadi insistently questioned the 'dharma of the ruler', everyone remained silent. Then Vidura scornfully spat out at the immorality of silence: when a crime occurs, he said, half the punishment goes to the guilty; a quarter to his ally; and another quarter falls on the silent.

Our Prime Minister's silence in the 2G scandal has been deeply disturbing. Soon after Raja announced his fraudulent policy in September 2007, the PM sensed that a crime of huge proportions was afoot. He wrote to Raja objecting to his policy, asking him to be transparent. Raja replied immediately, defending himself. On January 3, 2008, the PM acknowledged this letter-yes, 'acknowledged', as though he had acquiesced. This gave Raja the go-ahead to issue the licences. In May 2010, the PM admitted that Raja had indeed written to him. Why did the PM fall silent after having objected to the policy?

Raja has shamed us before the world. We, however, have always known the ugly truth: India's corruption begins when one is born — you have to bribe someone to get a birth certificate. It ends when one dies, when you are forced to 'buy' a death certificate. In between lies a dreary life of civic unvirtue, of continuous rishwat and *sifarish*. Founded on such high ideals, why is India so corrupt? There is nothing wrong with our genes. And the issue that Yudhishthira and Steinbeck have raised is a universal problem. You cannot blame parents for wanting children to grow up to be winners in life's rat race. But you can teach children to do the right thing — not to be silent when they see a crime. You can also reduce corruption by reform of the institutions of governance.

What makes Draupadi's question admirable is her insistence on dharma. Huge energies are spent on debates between the political Left and the Right when the real divide is between right and wrong conduct. Manmohan Singh understands this. This is why he promised to attack corruption through governance reforms in 2004 when he came to power. Reforming is never easy — it is like waging a war at Kurukshetra — but it must be done. The purpose of the Mahabharata's war, we discover at the epic's end, was to cleanse the earth which was groaning under the accumulated iniquity of its rulers. Our own rulers should prepare for the same fate as befell the sons of Bharata, unless they act now. The rulers of France also lost the faith of their people and suffered that fate in 1789.

Is the government giving licences to loot the public?

Shobhan Saxena | 19 January 2011

In the early 20th century, a British civil servant, posted in a dustbowl in central India, blew his top one morning when he noticed that his Indian servant hadn't polished his shoes properly. He called the servant, a young lad, and slapped him. Not satisfied with his explanation, the officer kicked him, punched him on the face and then slashed him with his leather belt. He kept beating him till he couldn't do it anymore — the servant was dead. After the poor Indian's wife and children wept and cried in front of senior British officers, the family was given Rs 25 in compensation. And the guilty officer was punished: he was made to pay Rs 25 in fine.

When I read this story in a school textbook many years ago, I was filled with anger. For days, I discussed the story with my classmates. We all agreed that the British were cruel by nature. That's why the British officer killed the Indian. In our hate-filled discussions, we completely missed the point that the British officer could get away by paying a fine of Rs 25. We completely missed the fact that in British India there were two sets of rules — one for the ruling class, comprising the British and their Indian collaborators, and another for ordinary Indians. The idea of justice was very simple: if a rich man was caught doing something wrong, he was fined; if a poor man was caught committing a crime, he was dumped into the jail.

More than 60 years after Independence, this colonial practice of letting the rich criminals get away with murder is still continuing. From two recent episodes it's become clear that we still have two sets of rules: one for the ruling class, another for the *aam aadmi.* Though the government has a list of 50 Indians who have illegal bank accounts in the Liechtenstein Bank in Germany, no action has been taken against these people. The government is treating the looting of money as a case of tax evasion and the culprits are being only fined despite the Supreme Court's observation that the government was "wrong in treating black money as a tax issue when it was simple and pure theft of the Indian economy". Criticizing the government for not making public all the names on the list, the apex court said on Tuesday that plunder of the nation had taken place.

Even if the Supreme Court didn't raise the issue, the Manmohan Singh government should have answered a few obvious and simple questions: Who are these people on the list? How many of them are in public life? What is the source of this money? Was public money siphoned off by these people? Why the government didn't make any attempt to recover this money?

But, instead of answering these uncomfortable questions, the government is busy shielding these criminals. Their identities have been hidden in a sealed envelope.

The second case which shows how the rich, famous and powerful of this country can get away with anything, particularly the plundering of national resources and public money, is the Lavasa hill station scandal. According to a report submitted to the Bombay high court on Tuesday, the Ministry of Environment and Forests has said that Lavasa Corporation violated environmental laws while building the hill station. But, instead of declaring the city illegal and order its demolition, the ministry has suggested a "hefty penalty and creation of a fund out of Lavasa's pockets to restore the damage done". By chickening out at the last moment, minister for environment Jairam Ramesh has proved that he is just a paper tiger who makes a lot of noise just for publicity. Recently, Ramesh had ordered the demolition of the Adarsh tower in Mumbai, but by giving the penalty option to Lavasa, he has unwittingly opened that penalty route to all criminals who are ravaging the country's eco-system in the name of development.

Because all these cases — Adarsh, Lavasa and Lichtenstein and Swiss bank accounts — involve the rich and powerful, no FIR has been filed till now, no one has been arrested, no body has been sent to jail and there are no indications that anyone would be prosecuted. If it was a case of theft in a rich man's house, the police would have picked some poor blokes, slapped cases against them and dumped them into jail in no time. There are more than 10,000 undertrials languishing in Delhi's Tihar jail. Most of them are in prison for petty crimes like pickpocketing or street fights. Most of them have spent more than seven years in prison, not because they have been sentenced by a court but because they don't have money for bail. And that's only one jail in the country. Hundreds of thousands of young men and women are rotting in jails because their families can't bail them out. In prison, many of them get raped or become drug addicts. If they come out after years in the company of hardened criminals, they become criminals too.

The government never bothers to save these young, innocent lives from going down the drain. Cabinet ministers don't act as lobbyists for these wretched souls. But, when it comes to acting against the wealthy, even if they are criminals, the state develops cold feet. Then it proposes the escape route: fine and penalty. That's what the Indian government has been doing in Lichtenstein and Lavasa cases. With details about Indians holding illegal bank accounts in Swiss banks likely to emerge soon, no points for guessing what the government would do. It will make sure that the identities of these criminals are protected and they get away by paying a fine. And the government would assure the corporates that their interests would be protected. Like everything else, our government is inspired by the US, the cradle of capitalism and its shady crimes. The famous mafia don of 1930s, Al Capone, was not arrested for years despite the fact that he openly ran dens of hooch, gambling and prostitution in the heart of Chicago. Because he bankrolled the politicians and bribed the cops, no one dared to touch him. Finally, when he became too big for his boots, they caught him, but not for his heinous crimes, including murder, but for tax evasion.

In predatory capitalism, criminals are allowed a free run as long as they pay their taxes. Not paying your taxes is the only crime in this system. And if you don't pay your taxes, you are doomed. That's why the Indian government is offering the tax route to the criminals who have stolen and stashed the country's public wealth abroad. That's why the government is happy with just levying a fine on the Lavasa corporation which has violated every rule in the book. And that's why it doesn't care for the poor people who keep rotting in prisons.

Support Anna, and all's changed: How naïve are we?

Anshul Chaturvedi | 17 April 2011

Everyone has a take on Anna. Here's my two penny worth: I think we're overrating things because we are so desperate to believe that drastic change is happening. An outside observer could be forgiven for believing that Jantar Mantar is the political equivalent of Tiananmen, that Delhi's fighting for change the way Cairo was a month back, and that there's a mass movement underway. During the days of Anna's fast, perfectly sane people have said stuff about how proud they are of Indian youth's "rising up" and how India is now almost the next Egypt.

Hello? It is one thing to dub the next T20 swashbuckler the next Viv Richards, or the latest kid on the cine block the next SRK, we like such flamboyance, but aren't we all in a bit of a collective overkill here? Haven't we been prone to waves of collective "all's changing" far too often to have forgotten them?

Though I wasn't quite in my teens then, the visible sense of positivity when Rajiv Gandhi first took oath after the 1984 elections was far too strong to not be noticed even by a school kid. Indira's assassination and the riots thereafter were hardly in the past, but even then, the overwhelming majority that Rajiv won — sympathy wave or not — gave a sense of the whole nation being together in this decision, in this formal anointment of a change of guard. And people liked Rajiv, they believed that he was, as the phrase went, Mr Clean. There were many, many people who thought that governance was headed for a basic change.

I was in high school when VP Singh ousted the Congress and rode to power in 1989, albeit with a very odd support mechanism of the right and the left, and for weeks, I recall, even my classmates wore Janta Dal symbols, the small green wheel, like badges on school uniforms, though our teachers frowned. *"VP tum sangharsh karo, hum tumhare saath hain"* was the refrain; it's of course been a common one since then, just the first name keeps changing. Everyone read the verdict in terms of the Bofors issue having lost Rajiv the prime ministership, and (though the Congress remained the single largest party) an anti-corruption crusader having been catapulted to national leadership. If I remember correctly, VP did things like flying by a regular airline flight as sitting prime minister – things that embedded themselves into the public mindspace when they happened. However, by the time VP had ridden out his 11 month tenure, the only thing most people knew him for was the Mandal Commission Report – and whether you loved or hated him depended on how you were impacted by his bringing in the quota.

When Vajpayee took over the reigns, and especially after the N-tests, there was a sense of national resurgence; I guess there is nothing like military accomplishment to make a country swell its collective chest. Vajpayee also happened to be the PM who faced the spectre of Kargil in response to his embracing Nawaz Sharif, and the subsequent Kargil war, besides perhaps doing for TV news in India what the Gulf War did for CNN in the US, again made us believe in things national; the fallen hero in battle makes you forget all else and think only of the collective entity for which he fell. The flag could make your hair stand on end and bring tears to grown men those days.

When people came out on the roads after 26/11, we all thought, and wrote effusively about, how the young want political change. How we will put up with nothing like this anymore, how we will all participate in change, demand greater accountabilty. How India can't put up with vacillating governance and public apathy any more. That was, of course, till the next time Mumbai went to vote in an election and about 52% people didn't turn up to vote.

The point is – we've been through euphoria many a time in the political lifecycle of the country, through events of perhaps greater or equal magnitude than the past few weeks, but they didn't bring drastic revolutions, or what they did achieve wasn't remotely as flamboyant or romantic as it appeared initially. Perhaps it's not an exact comparison, but when the Vajpayee regime thought India Shining made sense, most people didn't agree, or so the votes showed — and I do think that in personal credibility he at that time stood significantly stronger than Manmohan stands today. We, as a nation, are quick to paint rosy pictures that dominate the mindspace, but they may not necessarily change much on the ground, and may not even be believed by most — but few will say that, since that makes you a naysayer, a cynic, a disruptor of the mood of national euphoria, and so on.

I do not mean to be a pessimistic or a cynic, but, honestly, I find the great applause within middle class India for the 'victories achieved' a trifle overstated. Not that they don't mean much, not that Anna Hazare hasn't made a difference, not that he's not earned the respect and the credibility to make the government sit up and react — but we are so desperate as citizenry to believe that things are changing, the corrupt are on the back foot, that all's falling in place that we like to see it in far more romantic terms than the reality is. Twitter and Facebook do not, by themselves, a revolution make. Change is a systemic thing, a work of years, and very, very few among us are part of long term efforts and campaigns, at least not yet. Dare I say it, but the first time 90% of Anna Hazare's current crop of supporters began to support him in any coherent form was the day the Jantar Mantar fast began to make it to the media headlines. Now, Anna has been around many years, doing a lot. If his fast was in a village in interior MP, sans the TV cameras, well... We needed a face of credibility to speak against corruption, and Anna became that face for us, a rare man who has no baggage, who is not a fixer in politics. He fasts, we support his fast. Fair enough. Did we support him 5 years back? Will we support him 5 years hence? That, too, is relevant.

The point is not that we undermine or disrespect what has been achieved. The point is that if we accept this much as revolution, we'll sit back and relax, since we'll all have congratulated ourselves for the grand victory of civil society and convinced ourselves that now All Izz Well. These are structural, not fundamental, changes. We want a Lok Pal — but in a time when Chief Justices begin to come under the scanner as soon as they demit office, can we ensure Lok Pals will invariably be people whose integrity is above reproach?

Let's do a reality check. In the time elapsed since the World Cup final at Wankhede, India's had a revolution against the system, corruption is on a backfoot, we, the janta, have won? This is too easy. There's a long, long haul to 'winning' this; let's not delude ourselves so quickly, lest we begin to celebrate too early. Misplaced exuberance has been followed by lengthy disillusionments far too often. Let's keep our heads down and keep the pressure on, till things really, really begin to change. It's not going to happen in a matter of weeks. The victory celebrations, gentlemen, are a tad premature.

The Teflon Mr Pawar

Nauzer K Bharucha | 07 July 2010

The "breaking news" on TV was flashing Sharad Pawar's appointment as president of the International Cricket Council (ICC) when my wife came and whacked me on the head with the shopping bag. As I almost fell off the chair, she screamed, "French beans Rs 100 a kg, green peas at Rs 160 a kg, dal Rs 100 a kg. Does he now expect us to eat cricket balls?" she vented her frustration at India's agriculture minister, whose wide grin seemed somehow larger on the 37-inch LCD.

Surely, Pawarsaheb understands the travails of the common man, I assured her. After all, hasn't he already approached the Prime Minister to relieve him of some of his ministerial duties now that he has more weighty issues to worry about — like world cricket. The Maratha leader with a strong political base in the farming community knows a thing or two about crop patterns and foodgrain prices. And as a farmer himself, Pawar 'worships' land (and not necessarily the agricultural kind).

The Mr Teflon of Indian politics has had a long and often controversial association with matters pertaining to real estate. Those who tried to stick charges against him found the going tough. Like the former deputy commissioner of Mumbai's municipal corporation, G R Khairnar, who soon found himself suspended after levelling serious charges of corruption against Pawar, who was then Maharashtra's powerful chief minister in the mid-1990s. (The truckload of evidence that Khairnar had promised to produce never came, although the allegations saw the Congress government lose power in the state.)

If Pawar's current tenure as Union agriculture minister has left the Congress squirming (the alleged wheat scam that took place under his tutelage and rising foodgrain prices), his earlier avatar as Maharashtra's chief minister in the late 1980s witnessed a humungous 'land dereservation scam' in Mumbai. As many as 285 plots earmarked for various public amenities like parks, gardens, schools, hospitals and markets were dereserved by the Pawar government, leading to a major public uproar and charges of nepotism against the chief minister. The plots were to be parcelled off to builders for commercial exploitation. This was perhaps Pawar's first major brush with Mumbai's lucrative real estate and land deals. But more were to follow. When he was defence minister in the Narasihma Rao government, there was an audacious move to exploit the sprawling cantonment land in Pune for commercial purposes. Fortunately, it was nixed after the Army strongly opposed it.

Within Mumbai's building industry and in the corridors of power, Pawarsaheb's proximity to some developers and mega-projects is something that is widely spoken of. Among the most talked about connections is that with Lavasa, touted as India's most ambitious lake city complex up near Pune. Pawar's son-in-law, Sadanand Sule, had at one point in time held redeemable preference shares of Lavasa Corporation. Subsequently, the Sules got out of the project, but tongues still continued to wag despite strong denials about the family's involvement.

However, the latest revelation exposed Pawar's direct link with the Pune-based City Corporation — his family holds a 16% stake in the construction company controlled by his close aide Aniruddha Deshpande. Interestingly, in 2007, the Democratic Front government in Maharashtra, of which Pawar's NCP is a junior partner, came up with an innovative Special Township Policy. Not surprisingly, the first project to be approved by the government was the 400-acre Amanora Park township in Pune, which is promoted by none other than City Corporation. In Mumbai, the 5,500 acres of eco-sensitive salt pan lands are already seen having a huge real estate development potential despite vociferous protests by environmentalists. And guess who heads the group of ministers examining the unlocking of salt pan lands for commercial exploitation! The Teflon Mr Pawar himself.

Is it criminal to think small in India?

Gurcharan Das | 06 February 2011

There are two spaces in the politics of India. And one of them is empty. The two spaces reflect the classic division between those who look ahead and aspire versus those who look back and complain. Our political parties cater to the second — to the victim in us through their politics of grievance. The present gridlock in parliament is also a symptom of the same dispirited politics — no party is sufficiently hungry for reform to break the logjam. No one reflects the spirit of a rapidly growing India. Nor is anyone thinking big — and it's criminal to think small in India. Until the second space is filled, our politics will not be whole.

Congress appeals to the victim in the *aam admi* with an ever-expanding menu of job guarantees, food, gas and kerosene subsidies, and more. The BJP panders to the sufferer of historical Muslim misrule and to Congress' minority vote-bank politics. Mayawati and caste parties focus on the historical injustice to Dalits and OBCs. The Shiv Sena gratifies the injured pride of the *Marathi manoos.* All of this is about the politics of grievance and injustice.

India, however, is changing dramatically. It is nothing short of a miracle that it has become the world's second fastest growing economy in the midst of the most appalling governance. With high growth, mobility, and a demographic revolution of the young, Indians who aspire will soon overtake those who see themselves as victims. Pew surveys show that a majority of Indians believe they are better off than their parents and that their children will do even better. The person who got the 750 millionth phone number last month was a village migrant whose dream keeps slipping as his calls keep dropping partly because A Raja allegedly handed out the 2G spectrum in a corrupt fashion. India's 100 millionth internet user in 2013 will have information, which only the most privileged could access 20 years ago. No one in India's political life captures their hopes.

China's politicians do a far better job. While we debate if growth is pro-poor, China talks about growing rich. It understands that performance is a function of expectations. Those with higher expectations get higher performance. China no longer thinks itself a Third World country — it is challenging America today. In India, only a few politicians — Nitish Kumar, Sheila Dixit, and Narendra Modi — appeal to the aspirers. They speak the language of governance, roads and schools. But we need many more of them.

When I put this to a powerful Congress politician, he said that 'India shining' had died in the 2004 election. I gently reminded him that India's high growth economy had delivered 300 million into the middle class; another 250 million had been lifted out of poverty since the 1980s. So, a total of 550 million aspirers are surely worth fighting over. "Ah, but there are still another 550 million whiners, and their votes are more reliable than the shiners!" he said. If poverty were to magically disappear in India, the Congress party might lose its reason to exist.

Could the BJP become a party of aspiration? Vajpayee tried this when he unleashed the telecom and IT revolutions. His 'India shining' slogan did not lose the 2004 election — in fact, it was the defeat of key NDA allies in Andhra and Tamil Nadu. But even he could not shed Hindutva. There is no one today in the BJP who has the vision to discard the old baggage and convert it into a classic right-of-centre, secular party that stands single-mindedly for reforms and governance.

Aspirational politics would tackle our problems differently. Take, for instance, food inflation. The politics of grievance applies short term bandages — it tries to catch hoarders, stops forward trading, forbids export of grains when the country has had a bumper rice harvest and expects a record wheat crop (while ignoring Rs 17,000 crore of grains rotting under the tarpaulins of the Food Corporation of India or FCI). The politics of aspiration would recapitalize and reform agriculture and raise long-term supply — it would allow competition against the FCI in the warehousing of food, permit foreign investment in retail to establish cold chains, and allow farmers to lease their lands in order to raise productivity.

Who will fill the empty space in Indian politics? None of our parties understands that we live in a time of revolutionary change. Could it be Rahul Gandhi? So far he hasn't given any hint that he thinks big. India has doubled its cotton crop in the past five years, yet there have also been farmer suicides in cotton-growing areas. Both facts are correct. Rahul has chosen to focus on suicides. The future, however, will be built by those who focus on the first, who think big and give young Indians a sense of limitless possibilities.

What made Niira Radia so powerful

Kingshuk Nag | 14 December 2010

On a trip to Delhi late last year, I asked a friend knowledgeable about the goings-on in the corridors of power: "What's Niira Radia up to these days?" He laughed wrly: "Cabinet ministers may or may not attend meetings called by Manmohan Singh but if Niira calls for a dinner at her farmhouse, all ministers would be in attendance." He also said: "She's doing good, but with India-China business relations opening up, the lady is keen to catch this business as well. It seems that she knows the wife of a very important Chinese leader at a personal level."

Whether Radia was able to leverage this Chinese connection I do not know but clearly my friend's description was an exaggeration in the manner cartoonists emphasize a particular physical feature of their subject. Nonetheless, it demonstrated the importance of the lady in the power circles of Delhi.

The Radia tapes now demonstrate this truth starkly: how several top honchos in the media, business and government were eating out of her hand. The question is, what is the charm that the lady wove to make public figures so keen to gossip with her about important matters of the state and do her bidding or at least pretend to?

First, though styled a public relations consultant, Niira was only so in the broad sense of the word. She was a consultant with one foot in the corporate sector and the other in the government like virtually no one before in independent India.

In the good old days preceding liberalisation, there were liaison officers that corporates hired to remain on the right side of officers of the government or *netas.* They were low-profile: unseen and unheard of, and went about their jobs without much ado. Anyway, with the government and the public sector controlling the commanding heights of the economy, there was not much to do: getting some files cleared by the *babu* of the industry ministry, securing a purchase order from the DGS&D (directorate general of supply and disposal) or lobby with the finance ministry for duty change (import or excise duty or both) before the budget. Sometimes these liaison officers would get questions planted in Parliament through an obliging MP.

There were also public relations officers that corporates had on their rolls to write and disseminate press releases. These PROs had limited roles because the media was by and large shy of giving any publicity to private sector companies viewing this as needless advertising. Of course, there were full-fledged PR departments in public sector organisations that besides plugging for their chairmen and managing directors also performed sundry other work such as looking after company guesthouses.

Liberalisation brought about a sea change in the business environment. For the first time, public relation firms began to be established (actually the first ones came about just before the reforms process began). Corporates, all at sea in this new paradigm and apprehensive that their business would go down the tube in the new competitive environment, hired public relations companies that promised the moon in terms of build-up in the media. In reality, all they managed was to stand as middlemen between corporates and journalists. But that is another story.

Contrary to expectations, though liberalisation led to delicensing, it did not mean less of government. Now the private sector was being allowed into sectors hitherto out of bounds for the private sector, like power, mining, telecom and oil & gas. Industry-friendly policies were required for all these complex sectors about whose operations Indian *babus* had no idea. If not anything, then — from the point of view of industry — *babus* had to be educated, otherwise they would come up with "impractical" policies (at least in the details). This led to the birth of industry-specific organisations that lobbied for policy changes in specific sectors. It also led to the need for a new kind of professionals who would lobby for policy changes sought by individual corporates. Many public relations companies also mulled over diversifying into this business but most of them were deterred because this was a totally different ballgame.

It is at this stage that Nira Radia (she became Niira with a double "i" later, possibly for numerological reasons) burst forth on to the scene. This was the end of the 1990s. Having lived in London, she probably thought lobbying offered a great business opportunity. However, because lobbying was not considered a legitimate business, she set up a public relations firm with the Tata Group as her first client. The Tatas, with about 100 companies under their belt, offered considerable leverage to Radia. With her aggressive ends-justify-means approach, she was able to exploit this strength by selling unconventional ideas to her clients: like if the media gives bad coverage, stop advertising in the offending media. With the media business becoming more costly and cutthroat post-liberalisation, media organisations had to sit up and at least take note of this new reality. Radia, the perfect middlewoman, also portended to cut off access to her clients if you wrote anything uncomplimentary about them. That she practised these beliefs is apparent from her taped conversations: in one such conversation she threatens to boycott PTI! (Of course, this did not work out.)

It also goes without saying that with her smart and winning ways, Radia was able to charm at least some editors and was able to enlist the support of many journalists. This is besides many public figures who were ready to do business with her. For journalists looking for stories, with her (by now) extensive contacts, she was also able to supply great news material to them. As a result, many had virtually become supplicants to her. It won't be off the mark to conclude that at least some of them were on her payroll.

The government has said that it began tapping her phones because it suspected that she worked for some foreign agents. I doubt whether that is the case. But yes, with a lady with such extensive contacts it would make sense for them to engage her.

A tribute to whistle-blowers

Nauzer K Bharucha | 25 March 2011

"Can you meet me at Barista now? Make sure no one follows you," the shaky voice on the phone told me on a sultry April afternoon last year. He sounded nervous, but finally gathered the courage to meet me after much persuasion.

At the popular coffee shop outside the landmark Regal cinema in south Mumbai, Zende (name changed), a senior official of the city's electricity and transport undertaking (BEST), unravelled how the development rights of a prime bus depot plot was awarded to a developer, Indiabulls, at a throwaway price a few weeks earlier. As we sipped cold coffee, Zende betrayed a sense of constant anxiety, fearing he would be hounded and victimised by his seniors if found leaking information.

These are the brave anonymous and faceless whistle-blowers whom many journalists depend on for tip offs, just as the police bank on their informers. Based on Zende's information, The Times of India published a series of investigative reports over the next few days, which rocked the city and made the then chief minister Ashok Chavan (later caught in the Adarsh scam himself) intervene and order a probe into the land transaction. During this time, Zende took many risks in parcelling out sensitive documents to back up my articles. On one occasion, we met inside the leafy compound of an architecture college, eating Vadas in the canteen. His paranoia made him believe that his boss may be tapping his phone.

As in virtually all murky deals, the BEST had invited bids from builders to develop a strategically-located bus depot plot in Mumbai's western suburb of Santa Cruz. The tender document stipulated that bidders must quote a minimum price of Rs 369 crore, a figure that was arrived at by key officials after evaluating the value of this prime real estate.

Yet, barely two weeks before the bids were to be opened, the BEST administration suddenly decided to scrap this reserve price and allowed prospective bidders to quote any price they wanted. With barely four developers putting in their offers, the rapidly-growing real estate company Indiabulls got the development rights for just Rs 50 crore after it turned out to be the highest bidder.

The BEST Workers' Union described it is an "obvious scam". Chavan later told me that the transaction "sounds suspicious" and that he would get to the bottom of this controversy. When the CM finally ordered the inquiry, the BEST administration decided that it was no longer prudent to go ahead with processing the acceptance of Indiabulls' bid. It cancelled the land deal. Zende had a triumphant look when I met him again. "We need to celebrate this over beer," he said, before we parted. It's been over a year since then. Neither of us kept that promise.

Let 'butter' sense prevail

Vinita Dawra Nangia | 24 April 2011

Turn a situation on its head and make it work for you; don't melt under the expectations of others! Some conjectured that the Kerala CM V. S. Achuthanandan mixed up his kiddie advertising icons when he called Rahul Gandhi "Amul Baby". The ageing veteran surely meant Farex Baby, they snickered, not the "Amul girl"?! Or do you think he actually meant Murphy Baby, whispered some in a snide reference to his age. After all, Murphy baby in the 1960s would have been a more contemporary icon for the CM in his youth! Well, whichever baby he referred to, what was clear was the intent to insult. And Congress was quick to acknowledge the insult, with finance minister Pranab Mukherjee calling the remark "uncivilized" and others launching counter attacks on the CPM leader. Till Shashi Tharoor used his presence of mind and ready wit to turn the situation on its head. What's wrong with being an Amul baby, he tweeted. "Amul babies are fit, strong, focused on the future."

With that one tweet, Tharoor managed to inject lightheartedness into what had hitherto been a nasty situation between his political party and home state! And of course how could the dairy giant Amul, known for their witty billboards commenting on contemporary situations, resist the lure of an ad? They came out with an image of both politicians in dodgem cars, with the Amul girl as Rahul's companion, claiming, "They both are Amul Babies – Amul for young and old!"

Often we are at a loss how to react to a particular situation. At times like these, the weaker amongst us allow others and society in general to dictate our actions. This can lead to messy situations since we are responding to what others feel, not giving in to our own instinctive reactions! You may or may not feel insulted, but those around are eager to convince you of your humiliation! "How could he have insulted you like that! You must give it back to him!" Or, "Poor you, I can just imagine how you must be feeling. Don't worry, your time will come!" So much so that you are forced to stop smiling and start worrying about what exactly is wrong with you and how come you never noticed!

Before you let the reactionary rabble rousers take over, allow the Tharoor within you to take an unprejudiced, calmer and lighter look at the situation. Almost every situation can be turned on its head to be made to look shades better than what it seems at first sight. Not just look, but it can be made to act better for you as well. You can feel insulted or honoured, hurt or pleased, happy or sad, as it suits you. If you do not feel angry, who can ever manage to anger you? With control over the way you feel and react, you can manage the situation around you with incredible ease. And to hell with the way people imagine you should be reacting! Who out there really cares anyway? If Queen Kaikeyi had followed her instinct and stayed happy at her stepson Rama's ascension to the throne, she would have chosen a life of happiness and splendour for herself. Instead she allowed her insecurities to be fed by her maid Manthara, insisted on her son Bharata being crowned king and Rama being exiled; as a result she lost her husband Dashratha and ultimately died a lonely, brokenhearted woman with her son and daughter-inlaw (cousin of Sita) never forgiving her!

There are many Mantharas around, whose life's purpose is rabble-rousing, who go around feeding on others' misfortunes and exaggerating the same. Their position is dependent on those around them doing well or badly, and so they fire and fan emotions all around. Remember, once you let yourself be led by what they think you should be doing, these same people will also be the first to jump onto the other side and leave you alone. The only intelligent way to react to any situation is to examine it for its positive aspects and make the most of them. What cannot be changed need not be just endured, it can be enjoyed too! Being forced to work extra? Discover the fun aspects of that work and make the most of it! Overlooked for promotion at office? Enjoy another year honing your skills without the added responsibility. Nobody can keep a good man down for long! Beloved walked out on you? Maybe there's someone better waiting for you round the next corner...start looking! So if Rahul Gandhi was called an Amul baby, instead of reacting wildly and trading further insults, the best way was indeed to figure out Amul baby's good points and equate Rahul to those. After all, Amul means 'priceless' in Hindi! And isn't Rahul lucky the octogenarian politician didn't choose to compare him to the alien looking ZooZoos of the ballooned body and egg-shaped head instead! But what if he had? The ZooZoos too have their positive aspects! Ask Tharoor! He will tweet some more.

Good omens for rule of law in India

Gurcharan Das | 01 May 2011

On April 8, the day before Anna Hazare broke his fast, I was in Cairo to present the 'Indian model' for Egypt's future. After the conference, a few of us wandered off to Tahrir Square, where a massive demonstration had broken out. Through a twist of fate, I found myself suddenly on the podium, offering good wishes to the 37,000 protesters from the people of al-Hind. In the next three minutes I tried to convey a lesson from India's democracy: it is not elections, not liberty, not equality that finally matters; it is the rule of law. Corruption persists in India because the rule of law is weak.

That night, I woke to the sound of gunfire at 3 am. I thought they were firecrackers. There was a knock, and my host whispered that the army had moved into Tahrir Square and I should be prepared to flee as my 'three minutes of fame' was posted on YouTube. Filled with fear, I quickly changed, picked up my laptop and passport, and waited. I must have fallen asleep because the next moment it was 7 am and I was still alive. I saw a cloud of smoke above Tahrir Square and switched on the TV to learn that the army had left as quickly as it had come, leaving two dead.

I returned home much relieved. My Egyptian adventure made me view our own politics differently. Although I share Anna Hazare's rage against corruption, I feel ambivalent. However, the arrogant grandees of the political class, who from their private jets and black SUVs, are trying to smear his anti-corruption movement, have not understood the limited nature of political power in India.

India has always had a weak state and a strong society. Because political authority was either too distant or irrelevant to its daily life, we never allowed state power to be so concentrated, as in China, that it could reach deeply and change its basic social institutions. The type of despotic governments that emerged in China or Russia, which were able to divest the whole society of property and personal rights, have never existed in South Asia. Hence, India's history is of relative political disunity while China's is one of strong empires. Not surprisingly, India became a chaotic democracy after Independence. In the 1960s, Gunnar Myrdal called it a 'soft state'. Today, India seems to be rising from below, marching towards a modern, democratic and market-based future without too much help from the state. It is quite unlike China, whose success has been scripted from above by an amazing state that has built incredible infrastructure.

What is this society that has held India together for centuries? Jawaharlal Nehru defined it in three words: village, caste, and family. It consists of the over half-a-million autonomous, self-sufficient villages; more than 2,000 hierarchical jatis or sub-castes; and the joint family. What is significant is not hierarchy, as most think, but the idea that the group is more important than the individual. India's society is changing today, with power shifting from traditional to the civil society, including media.

The Indian state evolved from a tribal society, and the tribal raja's authority was limited by his kinsmen. The land did not belong to the king but to the clapn families. Even when sovereign states emerged in the 6th century BC, like Magadha, the king's power was limited by dharma or the law, and by the brahmin who interpreted the law. The law did not spring from the king as it did in China, but was above the monarch who was meant to protect it. The raja that violated dharma is called a mad dog in the "Mahabharata", and it calls for a revolt against him.

A successful nation must have an effective state and society. A weak state tolerates corruption, creates uncertainty in peoples' minds, and weakens the rule of law. People generally obey the law because they think that it is fair and applies to everyone equally. But if policemen, ministers and judges can be bought, people lose confidence in the rule of law.

The belated arrest of Suresh Kalmadi, the charging of Kanimozhi, and with A Raja already in jail — these are good omens for the future of the rule of law in India. It is now important to try and sentence the guilty speedily. The political class has stonewalled a Lokpal Bill for 40 years. Anna Hazare's original version was hugely flawed but with persistence we will soon have an effective law. A Lokpal Bill is not a panacea but it is a big step in the right direction. Meanwhile, I feel grateful that India has come a long way. Unlike Egypt, I do not have to fear the army, nor Islamists hijacking our secular democracy.

India must apologise to the Karmapa Lama

Shobhan Saxena | 18 February 2011

In the age of 24x7 TV channels facts are not sacrosanct and the only things that matter are screaming headlines, half-baked theories and silly opinions. The Karmapa affair is a good example of this malaise. Now the Union Ministry of Home Affairs has given a clean chit to the Karmapa Lama in the case involving seizure of foreign currency from 'his' monastery. But HP chief minister Prem Kumar Dhumal has refused to comment on the clean chit to the Karmapa, Ugyen Trinley Dorje, from the Central agencies which looked into the alleged violation of the Foreign Exchange Management Act by the Tibetan leader.

However, while speaking to some Tibetan reporters at Dharamsala on Thursday, Dhumal sang a diiferent tune. "Karmapa's name in any way is not involved in any land related cases. Neither there are any cases against some particular monastery person," said Dhumal. This is the same chief minister who has been going hammer and tongs at the Karmapa and the Dalai Lama and the entire Tibetan community in exile, making all kinds of wild allegations. To push his case, Dhumal even went to the extent of asking the Centre to reimburse the "entire amount of money spent by the Himachal government on the security of the Dalai Lama and Karmapa Lama". Now, it seems he has lost faith in his police but he won't admit it because the lies about the Karmapa have been repeated too many times.

Since lies spread faster than truth, these bizarre allegations against the Karmapa appeared in the media as the gospel truth. Stories coming from unnamed, anonymous sources were played on prime-time TV and splashed across the newspapers, leaving no doubt in some minds that the Karmapa was upto some mischief. First they blew smoke in the air and then began looking for the fire. With the state government and media hunting in pair, the Karmapa had no chance to prove his innocence. The Tibetan spiritual guru had already been declared guilty by suspicion. The entire Tibetan community in India had been put under the scanner.

The day the police raided the Gyuto Tantric Monastery in Dharamsala and allegedly found Rs 6 crore in possession of a resident of the monastery, TV screens were swarmed by conspiracy theories. Nothing was backed by facts. Truth was drowned in the cacophony of mindless allegations. If anything has been exposed by this unfortunate drama, it's the ignorance and gullibility of the Indian police and media.

Here is a look at some 'facts and evidence' which were either ignored or deliberately twisted by the media and their "invisible" sources to prove that the Karmapa was indeed a Chinese spy who had come to India to grab land across the Himalayan range on behalf of the Chinese government:

Chinese currency found at the monastery: It was alleged that the Karmapa is a Chinese spy because 1.1 million Chinese Yuan were found at the monastery. The police and media forgot to report that currencies of 25 other countries, including Taiwan, Japan, South Korea, UK, US, Australia, Thailand, Vietnam, Indonesia and Sri Lanka, were part of the cash found. Also, they ignored the fact that some travellers cheques were also found. They ignored this fact because it could prove that the money had come from hundreds of devotees from dozens of countries who visit the Karmapa every day, unless the police meant to accuse the Karmapa of working as a spy for all the 25 countries.

And it didn't occur to any reporter and investigator that the Chinese have to be very stupid to send their currency to the Karmapa. As it's not an international currency, the Yuan is just a piece of paper in India. One can't even buy a loaf of bread with it, forget using it for espionage. It's like sending an Indian spy to China with bundles of rupees. Plain stupid.

The Karmapa monastery is illegal: The DGP of Himachal alleged that the land deal for the Karmapa monastery proved that it was a 'benami property'. The allegation was parroted by the media without anyone pointing out that the Gyuto Tantric Monastery is neither owned nor constructed by the Karmapa. This monastery came up in the late 90s, years before Karmapa arrived in India. In fact, parts of the complex were still under construction when the Karmapa moved there in 2000. He lives in a small apartment on the top floor of this monastery and has nothing to do with the affairs of this institute. It's absolutely wrong to call it Karmapa's monastery. The Karmapa's monastery, Rumtek, is in Sikkim and he has been waiting for permission from the government of India to go there. Also, his application for building a monastery in HP is pending with the government.

He was sent to India by China: In 2000, when the Karmapa escaped to India, the Chinese claimed that he had gone to India to "collect some books and musical instruments". If he was their spy and his escape was stage-managed by Beijing, why would the Chinese be defensive on the issue and claim that he would come back to Tibet. It beats all logic. In fact, the Karmapa's escape was a huge embarrassment for China. It was the biggest escape from Tibet since 1959, when the Dalai Lama fled to India. It was the single biggest failure of China's policy in Tibet. To control the damage the Chinese floated a bizarre theory and we swallowed it hook, line and sinker . The Himachal police, which accused him of being a spy, hasn't produced a single piece of evidence, not even telephone call records, to prove that the Karmapa is in touch with someone in China.

Karmapa owns huge properties: One of the allegations made against the Karmapa was that he owns properties worth $1.5 million, including the Gyuto Tantric Monastery where he is staying at present. The fact that this monastery is not owned or built by the Karmapa was completely ignored. Also the fact that it was the Dalai Lama who had made arrangements for the Karmpapa to stay in two rooms at the top of Gyuto monastery was completely ignored. I have interviewed the Karmapaa at his residence a few times. It is a very small house with a small balcony. The police hasn't produced any evidence so far which suggests that the Karmapa owns properties worth $1.5 million in India. But this lie was flashed on TV screens as breaking news for days. And now Himachal CM says there's no case against the Karmapa.

He doesn't speak against China: One strong "evidence" against the Karmapa, according to his detractors, is that he hasn't said anything against China since he came to India. Again a total lie. In his first meeting with the press in 2000, the Karmapa had categorically said that he escaped to India because there was "no freedom in Tibet". In my interviews with him in the years 2000, 2001, 2004 and 2008, he spoke about issues of religious freedom and human rights in China. Of late, he has been repeatedly talking about environmental degradation in Tibet. As recently as December 8, 2010, I, along with some other journalists met the Karmapa at Bodhgaya and he again spoke about the problems in China-controlled Tibet. Also, his detractors forget a simple fact that the Karmapa is not a political leader but head of one of the four sects of Tibetan Buddhism, the Karma Kagyu sect. He is a spiritual leader. In the 1000 years of their history, the Karmapas have been entirely spiritual. The Karmapa is not supposed to talk about political issues. That role is reserved for the Dalai Lama who is the political leader of all Tibetans irrespective of their sects. We also never hear political comments from the heads of two other Tibetan sects, Nyingma and Sakya, but no one accuses them of being Chinese spies. So why single out the Karmapa?

The Himachal government has committed a Himalayan blunder by casting aspersions on the Karmapa in particular and the Tibetans in exile in general. Suddenly, there is a feeling among the Tibetans that they can't take their freedom in India for granted. This witch-hunt has rattled the community. So vicious were the attacks against the Tibetans that even the Dalai Lama, the most popular person in the world and India's best global ambassador, was accused by a nitwit of land grabbing. It was preposterous and stupid.

India should reassure the Tibetans that they are safe in this country and no political party will cut a deal with China for short-term gains at the expense of Tibetan refugees in India.

To begin with, the government must apologise to the Karmapa Lama.

Osama's death may end bloom of Arab Spring

SA Aiyar | 08 May 2011

I did not celebrate Osama bin Laden's death. Killing an individual is easier than killing an idea. Osama's idea of jihad survives his death.

He was the mastermind of 9/11 and the most iconic jihadi figure. Yet he had long ceased to direct jihadi movements and had run foul of some by killing Muslims opposed to al-Qaeda.

Nevertheless, Osama succeeded in popularizing a new version of jihad. In this, suicide attacks and civilian killings – both crimes in traditional Islam – became glorious jihadi tactics that fulfilled Islamic goals and ensured a passport to paradise.

John Brown, US anti-slavery leader, led a slave uprising in 1859, and was hanged for it. Yet his ideal of abolishing slavery triumphed. This inspired the US civil war song "John Brown's body lies a'mouldering in the grave, but his soul goes marching on." So too will Osama's.

His death may encourage the US to withdraw troops quickly from Afghanistan, strike a deal with the Taliban, and play down terrorism directed at India rather than the US. Pakistan will see this as vindication of its two-faced policy of using terrorists against India while playing footsie with the US. Such two-facedness may mean worse violence within Pakistan, with radicals gaining ground from liberal Muslims. India may suffer further 26/11-style attacks, more violence in Kashmir, and more external assistance for domestic jihadi groups. We may even suffer another Kandahar-type hijack.

To scotch this, militant Hindus want to emulate the US by raiding and assassinating targets in Pakistan such as Hafeez Saeed of the Lashkar-e-Taiba, mastermind of 26/11. This approach will fail. Just look at the ultimate failure of many killing missions of Israel, which is global No.1 in political assassinations and much admired for it by the RSS.

Ronen Bergman, Israeli military analyst, recalls that in 1992, Israel assassinated Hezbollah founder Abbas Mussawi. Far from weakening Hezbollah, this fuelled its anger and led to a retaliatory attack on the Israeli embassy in Buenos Aires, killing 29. Mussawi's replacement, Hassan Nasrallah, greatly increased Hezbollah's clout using arms supplies from Iran. This helped him wage an inconclusive war against Israel in 2006. Israel inflicted much damage on Lebanon, yet ended by withdrawing, a worse outcome than anything imaginable in Mussawi's time.

In 2004, Israel assassinated Hamas leader Sheikh Ahmed Yassin, hoping to cripple the organization. Instead, Hamas became stronger and more aggressive. Yassin was a devout Sunni who opposed Shia Iran, but after his death, Hamas happily joined hands with Iran and was armed by it, to Israel's utter dismay. So, while India faces a growing threat from jihadis, Israel shows us that assassination is no solution — it looks macho but ends up strengthening your foes. Ultimately, militant Islam will be quelled only by liberal Islam, not by outsiders, and that internal struggle is beyond our power to resolve. Whether we like it or not, we cannot impose a military solution.

Optimists disagree. They claim that jihad as a philosophy has been beaten back by the Arab Spring, and that secular freedom movements in Egypt, Tunisia and Libya have displaced sectarian ones. I would love to believe this is the case, but history suggests otherwise.

Many liberals (including me) hailed the 1979 Iranian revolution that overthrew the Shah. Alas, this brought not democracy but a murderous, oppressive theocracy.

Liberals cheered prospects of democracy when Algeria held its first free elections in 1991. But an Islamist party won the first round. So, with US blessings, democracy was abandoned in favour of continued military rule. Elections in Palestine brought to power Hamas, a radical Islamic party, humiliating the secular PLO.

Why do Islamists so often win free elections in the Middle East?

Because local dictators can neuter secular opposition groups but dare not close down the mosques. Hence mosques become natural opposition centres. When autocracy gives way to elections, Islamic parties (like the Muslim Brotherhood) are the best organized, and so best placed to win. In Egypt's referendum on constitutional reform in March, opposition leader El Baradei (who wanted elections put off to help secular parties organize) was prevented from casting his vote by Islamists who pelted stones. Does this portend liberal democracy or Islamist intolerance?

This must stoke fears that the Arab Spring will bring radical Islamists to power in many countries. I would love to be proved wrong. But I have a sinking feeling that we will soon say of Osama what Bertold Brecht said of Hitler.

"Don't rejoice in his defeat, you men.
For though the world stood up and stopped the bastard,
The bitch that bore him is in heat again."

Jihad lives on after Bin Laden

TK Arun | 02 May 2011

The terrorist has been killed but the ideology of terror he championed lives on, in multiple organisations and individuals, in different parts of the world. Osama bin Laden was the most potent symbol of the ideology of terror in the name of Islam, and its destruction is, indeed, a severe setback for the movement. However, in an attempt to prove that a symbol's fall does not mean defeat of what it stood for, al Qaida and its ideological affiliates are likely to stage reprisal attacks around the world, seeking American targets, but not just American ones. India needs to be doubly vigilant.

The Pakistani establishment finds itself not just discredited, but in double jeopardy. It is improbable that Osama bin Laden could have sheltered himself in a huge mansion with barbed-wire-mounted 17 ft walls in one of Islamabad's poshest suburbs without the Pakistani authorities' knowledge and consent. This makes the Pakistani establishment — the army and the Inter-Service Intelligence, more than the toothsome yet toothless civilian government — deeply suspect in the eyes of all those fighting terror. If this is not bad enough, the army and the ISI are now likely to face charges of betrayal and sell-out by various terror groups. If the Pak military authorities profess they did not actively participate in the American operation to attack the compound and kill its inmates, the terrorists would find it difficult to believe that the Pak brass did not at least know in advance about the impending attack, notwithstanding express denial by the Americans of any prior notification of Pak authorities. Can a number of helicopters fly into and across Pakistani airspace without detection? If they could, what kind of security does the Pakistani armed forces offer their countrymen? If detection was inevitable, the only plausible explanation for the army/ISI failure to at least tip off bin Laden is that Islamabad both sheltered bin Laden and then later betrayed him, when it was convenient to perform either act of perfidy. This means that no self-respecting group can trust the Pak army or ISI anymore.

What this does is not just to put a crimp on the Pak army's ambition of using terror for strategic depth but also to deepen the crisis in Pakistan's polity. Pakistan's options are narrowing further and further to real, substantive, broadbased democracy, in which real power would have to be transferred from the army to the people.

Cometh the hour, cometh the man — so they say. It sometimes works the other way round, too. Goeth the hour, goeth the man. Islamic radicalism was inspired as much by the absence of democracy in the core Islamic countries led by Saudi Arabia, and absence of any forms of legitimate redressal of popular grievance. The ongoing movement for democracy in the Arab countries opens a huge window of opportunity to achieve freedom and choice through legitimate means, leaving violence out of the picture. For these movements for democracy to achieve lasting success, the rest of the world would have to cooperate to see democracy established in Saudi Arabia, and a viable state of Palestine that offers Israel security as well.

Questions for Pakistan

Indrani Bagchi | 03 May 2011

Pakistan was caught red-handed with Osama bin Laden on Sunday as a top-secret, Hollywood-style US operation killed the world's most wanted terrorist in a mansion near Islamabad. Exposed and embarrassed, Pakistan finds itself in a cleft stick. Bin Laden's hideout, a stone's throw away from the elite Pakistan Military Academy, has raised questions about Pakistan's involvement in sheltering Bin Laden for 10 years when the whole world was looking for him.

Pakistan will now have to answer questions, how much did they know about Bin Laden's whereabouts and how long were they sheltering him? Most important, why were they sheltering Bin Laden, if they had such a strategic partnership with the US? Pakistan has taken over $20 billion from the US for the past decade for the war in Afghanistan which was centred around the capture of Osama bin Laden and disruption of Al Qaeda. By playing such a high stakes double game, Pakistan is in danger of eroding what little relationship they had with the US. It will make it more difficult for the US to use the fig leaf that Pakistan is "cooperating fully" on terrorism.

Pakistan media is asking more searching questions. Dawn, for instance, says it was really strange that a normally paranoid military and intelligence setup would not have made enquiries about an unusually highly secured compound 800 metres from their version of West Point. ISI would have had detailed dossiers on all the residents in the area. ISI officials are apparently claiming an "intelligence failure".

To add to the conspiracy mills, the Dawn correspondent says, "Was the general completely unaware that the most wanted man lived but a short distance away? Did he also not have a clue about what was to happen in the coming days in that town?" In retrospect, he says, there were signs that something was up.

ISAF Commander Gen Petraeus paid an extraordinary visit to Islamabad last Monday (April 25), when he is said to have held 'a short and crisp' discussion with Gen Kayani at an unusual meeting venue — Chaklala Airbase. The two generals are even said to have taken a short trip to an undisclosed location on board an aircraft. The same night Gen Petraeus had through teleconferencing attended a White House meeting chaired by President Barack Obama.

"Observers feel that President Obama referred to that meeting in his speech on Monday morning, in which he announced the death of Osama: "And finally, last week, I determined that we had enough intelligence to take action, and authorised an operation to get Osama Bin Laden and bring him to justice."

The very next day, Pakistan's top military coordination body — Joint Chiefs of Staff Committee — held its quarterly session, which was attended among others by ISI Chief Gen Shuja Pasha, who otherwise isn't a regular member of the body. The meeting was unscheduled.

Another anomaly in the Pakistan military's account of the raid is their explanation of how four US helicopters evaded the country's air defence system for about an hour (almost 30 minutes each side) as they flew in from Bagram and returned after a 40-minute long foray.

One official claimed that the helicopters succeeded in avoiding detection through 'Nap of the earth flight' — a military tactic involving low-altitude flying to evade air defence systems. Yet another maintained that the air defence systems had been jammed by the Americans."

It left Pakistan army embarrassed and exposed, prompting different uncoordinated reactions from different parts of the establishment. While the ISI claimed prior knowledge, with DG ISI and other retired military commentators saying they were part of it, the civilian government made no bones about their ignorance.

It leaves Pakistan with an unenviable choice — by claiming knowledge, they would be opening themselves up for reprisal attacks from Al Qaeda or its affiliate groups. Claiming ignorance would expose them to the charge from various quarters in Pakistan that they could similarly allow US access to their strategic assets – nuclear weapons. For all the terrorist leaders and Taliban that remain under their protection, they may be convinced the ISI could betray them to the US as well in future.

Pakistan will most likely suffer severe reprisal attacks from Taliban groups closely associated with Bin Laden, as well as Al Qaeda. Simultaneously, Pakistan can expect to see increased international pressure to give up other global terrorists under their protection – Mullah Omar, Ayman Zawahiri, Quetta shura... the list could go on. Pakistan's deteriorating condition will also make it very difficult for them to resist the pressure. This could lead to a more vicious cycle of blowback attacks from these groups.

The most powerful man in the world

CP Surendran | 10 December 2010

The most powerful man in the world is not Barack Obama. It is Julian Assange, WikiLeaks founder, who is making America think again about big words like democracy and free speech, the kind of stuff that country prided itself on.

Allegedly Assange is promiscuous. There are rape cases filed against him. Since he is one way or the other stealing information that the US government considers classified, he could be called a thief. And since what he does can be easily interpreted as seditious, he could have been accused of treason if he were a US citizen. Enough stuff then to put him behind bars or keep him on the run. In short, a man of many failings. Just like you and me.

Yet news about him drives newspaper sales. Every time WikiLeaks puts out apparently sensitive documents, the print world follows up on the act and in the short term at least does well. You could be forgiven to think that on a good day the net is print's benefactor.

Washington has done all it can to shut down WikiLeaks' operations. But the leaks keep popping up on mirror sites. There are any number of online debates and discussions happening on WikiLeaks. Most of them seem to think this is a clash between cultures, of the new net-based and truly democratic generation and the old posers in power, who mouth the good words and then pull the trigger.

Maybe it is. Equally, it is how the balance of power is shifting back to the individual in his fight against the system, here the state itself.

Assange is powerful, because like Mahatma Gandhi, he is using truth as a strategic weapon. But unlike Gandhi, he has the unique advantage of the net, one of the most democratic of technologies. The US is a technologically driven country. It's perhaps justice then that it has met its match in a man who knows how to use technology with such subversive impact.

That Assange can disprove stated positions of a superpower and hold it accountable to its actions virtually single-handedly is good news to all those who believe patriotism and national identities must be subservient to human rights and ethics. The first is politics. The second is poetry. The individual is finding his voice again. And he is forcing the system to respect him. The power of one is now. And Assange is the man.

Tragic triumph

Jug Suraiya | 15 March 2011

Can Japan triumph in tragedy? Japanese Prime Minister Naoto Kan has described the catastrophic combination of earthquakes, tsunami and nuclear meltdown as the biggest crisis the country has had to face since the end of World War II which was brought to an apocalyptic end with the atomic fireballs mushrooming over Hiroshima and Nagasaki. The bombs — codenamed Fat Boy and Thin Man — took a death toll of between 1,50,000 and 2,40,000 human lives; nature's fury has claimed over 10,000 victims, showing that at its very worst the destructive force of the natural world is far surpassed by the deadly ferocity of man's violence against man.

The economic loss caused by destruction of property and infrastructure cannot even begin to be calculated as yet. In the midst of this appalling devastation it might seem like an obscene joke to suggest that a tragedy of this magnitude could possibly be turned eventually into a triumph.

Yet curiously enough, time and again, not just the human spirit but also the laws of economics have proved amazingly resilient in the face of the most terrible of adversities, when widespread destruction has been taken as a challenge and an opportunity to rebuild with renewed enterprise and determination. The Gujarat earthquake of 2001 is an example. Surat, which was almost totally destroyed in the quake, sprang up out of the killer earth in a rejuvenated avatar, cleaner, better planned and more prosperous than ever before. Indeed, some might attribute the rise of Gujarat as an economic super-state more to the seismic upheaval than to Narendra Modi.

In a paradox that is both cruel and kind, destruction spurs

reconstruction and acts as a stimulus for economic enterprise. Surveys have shown that, more often than not, stock markets which crash immediately in the wake of a catastrophe tend to gain new highs shortly after as work of rebuilding begins, generating large-scale production and employment.

History reveals many such examples. The great fire which destroyed almost all of London in the 17th century — an eyewitness account of which is vividly presented in Samuel Pepys's famous diary — turned out in the long run to be more of a blessing than a bane. The conflagration scoured the city of the filthy, crowded hovels which were inevitable breeding places for plague-carrying rats and other disease-bearing vermin. Rebuilt, London came into its own as one of the biggest and richest cities in the world. The gilded Monument in the City of London commemorates the Great Fire and its triumphant aftermath.

Similarly, the great fire that engulfed Chicago in 1871 — caused according to folklore by the twitching tail of a cow which knocked over an oil lantern and set ablaze a pile of hay — was seized by the 'City of Broad Shoulders', as poet Carl Sandberg would later describe it, as an opportunity to recreate itself in a new, innovative image. Their thriving city of cattle stockyards and grain silos reducing to smouldering ruin, Chicago's civic leaders invited architects from the world over to submit their most imaginative designs for its rebuilding. That's how what was billed as the world's first 'skyscraper' — at that time, a building 10 storeys tall — came up in Chicago, renowned today both for its robust local economy and the elegance of its architecture.

Japan itself — the only country in the world to have been the target of not one but two nuclear attacks — rose phoenix-like out of the ashes of a world war and went on to become a globally acclaimed 'economic miracle', the Land of the Rising Sony, a synonym for inventive industry. Today, Japan is once again a deeply wounded victim of malign forces. Will it once again overturn disaster into remarkable victory? It can and it will, because it must. Not just for its own sake, but for the sake of that single fragile and yet indestructible bond that links humankind together: a bond and a lifeline called hope.

Stop this futile Pak bashing

TK Arun | May 05, 2011

Pak perfidy is now the big thing for Indian media, from calls to dump the Mohali spirit and rants against the Pak policy of hunting with the hounds while providing safe burrows for hares to wild hopes that Washington will now declare Pakistan a new enemy. The impact, if any, of this frenzy on Pakistan would be counterproductive: to whip up nationalist fervour and impede internal reform.

Does anyone who wasn't born yesterday need Osama bin Laden being tracked down to a mansion near Rawalpindi to be convinced of Pakistan's reliance on terror as an instrument of state policy? Pakistan recruited, trained and armed the Taliban. Ditto for terrorists targeting India. The Americans handed over to India transcripts of the instructions flowing out of Pakistan to the terrorists who attacked Mumbai in 2008. Who does not know, except for those who choose not to know, like China, of Pakistan's comfort with the proposition that terror is war by other means? The question is, what can India realistically do about it? War or surgical strikes or daring raids of the kind American Navy Seals performed to take out bin Laden are not viable options, given the real possibility of such actions' swift escalation into a nuclear confrontation.

What has really changed after bin Laden's elimination? The most important factor is the serious blow it has delivered to the legitimacy and prestige of the Pak army. If the Pak army and its intelligence wing knew nothing about Osama having taken shelter in a suburb of Islamabad, and this state of blissful ignorance extended to the incursion of American helicopters into Pak airspace and a 40 minute firefight close to a military installation, then the army's competence is zilch. If, on the other hand — and this is a more likely contingency — if the Pak army knew what was going on, both when bin Laden found a safe house near Islamabad and when American special forces killed him, it is a treacherous force that cannot be trusted by friend or foe. Friend can turn foe or a seeming foe actually be a friend. In other words, on account of either trustworthiness or competence, the Pak army is the pits.

This loss of credibility has serious implications for the Pak army's ability to use terror as a means of strategic depth. No terror outfit can any longer swear to love, honour and obey the Pak army as in the past. Depending on the constellation of international pressure and domestic politics, the army could wash its hand of any group it had been supporting, at any point of time. A dead Osama bin Laden is living testimony to the Pak army's fickle fidelity.

But don't police informers and double agents work under such perilous patronage all the time? Why should terror outfits alone be put off by such unreliable sponsorship? The difference is in the nature of the motivation. Informers and the like work for money, and accept the risks as they come. Terror groups are driven by ideology, commitment to what they believe to be a calling as high as the heavens. Those who betray such committed soldiers also betray the larger cause and cannot be pardoned. The irrationality that drives their commitment and cohesion makes terrorists difficult customers when it comes to accommodation within a framework of cold-blooded calculus of the kind the Pak army would seem to have employed with regard to bin Laden.

The army's loss of prestige and weakened ability to deploy obedient dogs of war would be the two concrete outcomes of the bin Laden killing that India has to factor in. The continuing movement for democracy in the Arab world is another. India has good relations with all the regimes that are under threat from their own people. So it is difficult to support movements whose eventual success can only be speculated on, against entrenched governments. Yet, India must throw in its lot with the people, not with the governments. Modernity and democracy in the Islamic world will not just make jihad redundant but also make it difficult for Pakistan's oligarchy to continue the pretend that they have a democracy going over there. Radical internal reform is Pakistan's route to emancipation from a national self-definition in hostility to India, and to civilian supremacy over the military establishment.

Pak bashing in India only serves to unleash defensive nationalism in that country, hampering internal reform and restoring lost legitimacy to the army. The sensible course for India is to continue to engage the state, such as it is, in Pakistan, while encouraging democracy and reform in the Arab world. And the latter would be incomplete without an independent state of Palestine at peace with Israel.

In return for its cooperation in supporting democracy in the Arab world, India should ask the US to not let Afghanistan relapse into Taliban rule, however distrustful the Taliban might now be, of the Pak army. This would be a constructive response, not high-decibel Pak bashing.

Dump opium in Afghanistan, bankrupt Taliban

SA Aiyar | 20 February 2011

One reason for the Taliban's resilience in Afghanistan is the big money they make from the opium trade. Attempts to cut off external financing for the Taliban have failed since it generates so much money within the country.

The US has tried destroying the poppy crop. It has tried to use friendly mullahs to denounce opium as un-Islamic. It has sought to promote grapes, saffron and high-yielding wheat as alternatives to poppy. None of these approaches has worked. In despair, some analysts want the US to buy the entire poppy crop in Afghanistan, and then destroy it.

All these approaches are escapist, and fail to come to grips with ground realities. The Afghan government barely exists in much of the country, and many officials in rural areas are corrupt or in league with the Taliban. They cannot be depended on to destroy the poppy crop, not even with support from US helicopters. Many Afghans admit that drugs are un-Islamic, but the profitability of poppy cultivation has easily overcome their moral scruples, especially since the damage is ultimately inflicted on white infidels in distant lands.

Since all proposed remedies so far have failed, we need to think out of the box and come up with a totally new approach. Forget any military or religious approach to the problem. Instead, let us understand what the laws of supply and demand imply in the opium context.

To produce opium, Afghan farmers lance poppy plants, and

painstakingly collect the latex that oozes out. The dried latex is called opium. It contains up to 12% morphine, along with codeine and alkaloids such as thebaine and nocapine. Morphine, codeine and other processed alkaloids have medical uses as painkillers. But drug lords process these alkaloids into heroin, and sell this highly addictive drug at sky-high prices on western streets.

Opium production is banned globally, save in India where it is produced on regulated farms under government supervision. Most opium production is illicit, and Afghanistan accounts for nine-tenths of it. The Taliban levy atax on Afghan farmers and also buy opium to be processed and smuggled abroad.

Turkey was once a major opium producer, but banned it many years ago. Turkey and Australia now grow poppies under government regulation, but they do not use the manual route of lancing poppies and scraping off the ooze. Instead they mechanically harvest the entire poppy crop. This is called poppy straw, and it is then chemically processed to extract medical alkaloids like morphine.

Some international medical groups have complained that there is a global shortage of medical morphine, and that Africa in particular is condemned to needless pain for want of enough morphine. These groups believe the right approach is for the US to buy up the whole Afghan poppy crop and process this into morphine for medical use. Many hard-headed military and policy experts also think this can be an effective way of depriving the Taliban of opium income.

Problem: these experts are ignoring basic economics. Today, the Afghan poppy crop is grown mainly in southern provinces like Helmand. If the US or some medical council tries to buy up Helmand's poppy production, opium will become scarce in the black market and prices will skyrocket. This will induce other provinces to take up poppy cultivation. Indeed, cultivation will also spread rapidly to neighbouring countries (Iran, Pakistan, Turkmenistan, Uzbekistan and Tajikistan) and the resultant opium will be smuggled into Afghanistan. The Taliban will, of course, profit handsomely from this illicit trade.

Basic economics says that any strategy that makes opium scarce will fail, since it will encourage further cultivation. The solution lies in increasing the supply of opium so greatly that its price crashes, making cultivation unprofitable.

How can we achieve this? The US could ask Australia to licence a big jump in poppy straw production, guaranteeing to buy and process the entire production into opiates. These opiates could then be dumped in Afghanistan. Afghan opium prices will crash and farmers will turn to other crops.

An alternative strategy could be for the US to legalize drug use. Once heroin becomes legal, its street price will plummet, and so will the Afghan price. However, political and religious opposition to legalizing drug use in the US is very strong. There will be much less opposition to dumping opiates in Afghanistan. Indeed, US farm belt legislators may even suggest poppy cultivation (with safeguards) in the US, providing farmers with a lucrative new crop.

Crown and country

Jug Suraiya | 05 May 2011

In the event, I didn't go to the WillKat wedding. For one thing, I read somewhere that the couple were going to be serving wine and champagne at the event but no beer. Why? Because beer – unlike wine and champagne – is seen to be a drink of the working classes. Beer at a Windsor at-home? Good lord. Mummyji would get her tiara, not to mention other things, in a right royal twist.

The other reason that I didn't go is that over the years I've developed an allergy to any form of royalty. Some people are allergic to peanuts, or prawns, or dairy products. If, by mistake, they ingest one of these things their faces swell up, or they break out in spots. In my case, my allergy to royalty causes me to break into a sneezing fit, often at the mere mention of a member of the species.

It first manifested itself years ago when I knew a Calcutta family the head of which had in his youth been an ADC to a Rajasthani maharaja. Every now and then, in the course of general conversation (So hot and sticky the weather is, no?), mention would be made of the maharaja connection whereupon the entire family would apparently be seized by a collective fit of sneezing, all of them going Ziness!, Ziness!, Ziness ! Bless you, I'd say to them. Bless you, bless you.

One day, one of them asked me: Why do you keep saying bless you? Because you keep sneezing all the time, I replied, and demonstrated how they did it: Ziness! We're not sneezing, you idiot, I was informed. We're referring to His Ziness, the Maharaja.

It seemed that, in royal circles, the preferred pronunciation of 'Highness' – as in 'His Most Royal and Exalted Highness' – was 'Ziness' with an exclamation mark at the end and an accompanying clicking together of heels. I don't know if it was that particular experience or something else, but I start sneezing when people start talking about royalty. Reason I don't play cards. Can't, what with all those kings and queens mucking about.

Anyway, I'm glad that the WillKat nuptials went off without any glitches, or sneezes. Though it all seemed pretty tame stuff, no drama-*baji* like we have in Indian weddings. No last-minute dowry demands. No *bhangra-ing baratis*. No helicopters. No shotguns fired into the air, bringing down the stray crow or curious bystander caught in the blast. No wailing pooh-paah cars competing with the wailing of shehnais. No Bollywood starlets doing item numbers.

Still, it was a nice *shaadi*, and I wish the couple all the best for the future. As and when Mummy*ji* finally steps down, and Charlie-baba ascends to the throne — How will they get him out of the wheelchair and onto it? — Willie will be next in line to be king. Perhaps it's time he began to take a few kingly lessons. True, he'll be king of only a small, wet island largely inhabited by Pakistanis and Bangladeshis who run *balti* restaurants the waiters of which are rumoured to spit in cheery contempt into the chicken tikka masala that the natives consume with obsessive dedication. But a king's a king for all that, and a little royal tutoring might well be in order. Where should Willie go to get it?

Ever since the French Revolution, royalty keeps a low profile in Europe. As in the case of the midget monarch, Sarkozy I of France, who stands five-foot nothing in his elevator shoes. With the Indian takeover and the booting out of the poor Chogyal, royalty has been banished from Sikkim, as it has from Nepal following popular demand. Bhutan's King Jigme Wangchuk has stepped down for his son (why won't Mummyji take a hint?) and has also announced a rollout plan for democracy. The anti-royal Jasmine Revolution is sweeping West Asia and North Africa. So where can poor Willie go to learn to be a proper monarch? Which is the only country left in the world where dynasty is destiny, and destiny is dynasty?

All right Willie, pop across and we'll try and arrange to get you a darshan of a truly Royal Family. OK, Maharani Soniaji, Yuvraj Rahulji? Ziness! (Damn, there goes the sneezing again.)

We don't need an Osama to destabilise us

Rajesh Kalra | 04 May 2011

This is not yet another post on Osama bin Laden or Pakistan or how the United States is strong and we are weak or whether we should now obliterate Pakistan if it refuses to part with Dawood. This is, in fact, yet another post about the plummeting respect for law, absence of fear for law enforcement and all else.

Just move away from the series of scams that have exploded in our faces these past several months and you would think that it can't get any worse. Perhaps the incidents that I am about to share may look puny in comparison. However, looked at in totality, they do convey the extent of the rot that has engulfed our system.

Look at the two SMSs I've received these past few months. One was received a few months ago and the second just a few days ago.

In all our urban areas, it is an open secret that municipal authorities or town planners are a law unto themselves. The haphazard manner in which our urban growth is taking place is testimony to that. An architect friend of mine in Delhi always tells me that if you are willing to spend enough, he can get a blank sheet approved and make a drawing on it later. One had, however, felt that after the nation's apex court got into the act to strictly enforce laws, things would have gotten better. There is also this fear of the authorities sealing any unauthorised construction. We also know that with some hefty *chai paani*, it is possible to wriggle out of such situations, but it was always done quietly, discretely. Not any more, as this SMS that I received would prove.

Now switch to the modern day bug bear of all mobile users — hundreds of unsolicited messages and phone calls all through the day. Remember there is a DND (Do not disturb) registry that, once you have registered in, is supposed to put an end to this virus. You would also remember how successive regulators and ministers have promised to end this menace, only to back off at the last moment. And look at a message I received recently.

What I am trying to tell you is that the little bit fear, or shame that anyone had about taking on the law or fear for it has almost evaporated. Only the poor and the common man, to an extent, still worries a bit about something called rule of law. All others have resorted to complete brazenness in their actions.

All those living in urban areas can often see advertisements that invite students to their centres with catchlines such as: 9th fail. Apply and get 10th certificate or 12th pass, get a BA degree. But honestly, why blame these alone, who must be operating under the patronage of some bigwig corrupt *neta-babu* nexus. Isn't this just a spec of what else is being witnessed all the time? What about the fake pilots. I would rather have a 9th fail get a 10th certificate than a commercial pilot's license or a medical degree. Settle for the lesser evil when its inevitable.

What does this all show? It shows a complete breakdown of law and order and total absence of fear of both law and enforcement agencies. They mock at the law and law enforcement agencies and all else. Not too long ago we used to say, our corrupt politicians have corrupted institutions. All that has now transformed and we have now reached a stage where these worthies have institutionalised corruption.

The CVC recently came out with another report saying the bridges built for the Commonwealth Games used substandard material and are dangerous. The political response was that they would once again examine the quality and then, perhaps thrash the CVC report. All those who have been arguing that CVC is enough to tackle corruption among *babus* and there is no need for a stronger body with powers to punish must look at this case closely to see how powerless, toothless this body is.

Ultimately, it is we, the people, who have to wake up. The realisation has to come from within. Unless we do that, these canny corrupts would not stop till they have made a mincemeat of us and our nation. One may not be able to see though now, but this has the potential of destabilising our fabric more than anything else. Other nations may have required an Osama to destabilise them. We seem to be doing so without his assistance.

Wimpish India may lose the Great Game

Swapan Dasgupta | 08 May 2011

A week after 9/11, when an angry United States was planning fierce retribution against Osama bin Laden and his Taliban hosts, General Pervez Musharraf made a televised speech on the choices facing Pakistan. In a rambling address, Musharraf drew inspiration from the early history of Islam. The Prophet, he reminded viewers, had negotiated the Treaty of Hudaibiya with the Quraish of Mecca. The truce may have seemed a climb down and an admission of weakness but it offered the army of Islam the elbow room to spread the faith throughout the Arabian Peninsula. It was an invigorated Islam that finally regained Mecca.

The implication was obvious: confronted by a superpower that bluntly demanded Pakistan should choose between Us and Them, Musharraf was effecting a tactical retreat. To Musharraf, the U-turn in Afghanistan didn't signal any strategic shift or emotional conversion; it suggested dissimulation based on expediency – the al *taqiyya* or deception that is theologically sanctioned for the larger good of the faith.

With the encounter in Abbottabad ending an exhaustive manhunt, there must be functionaries in Washington DC who regret not being more attentive to the fine print of Musharraf's September 2001 speech. It is not that the US and its allies weren't aware of Pakistan's penchant for "looking both ways" and facilitating Taliban factions. But its duplicity was sought to be rationalized as wariness of a regime in Kabul that valued India. As the relationship with

President Hamid Karzai began souring, it suited western strategists to imagine that Pakistan's shenanigans were facets of a new Indo-Pak proxy war. With war weariness engulfing the public mood in both the US and Britain, 'pragmatism' deemed that Pakistan should have a major say in determining a peace settlement that included the Taliban — as distinct from the Al-Qaeda. In a speech in February this year, US secretary of state Hillary Clinton even deemed that laying down of arms and acceptance of the Afghan Constitution were no longer prerequisites for dialogue with the Taliban.

Until the May 2 "firefight" spoiled the party, Pakistan believed it was on the cusp of a historic victory. With President Barack Obama having announced a phased withdrawal of US forces from July, Islamabad felt it was just a matter of time before it regained its "strategic depth" in Afghanistan. Its army chief General Kayani was audacious enough to suggest to Karzai last month that his cooperation in a settlement that accommodated the Taliban could even be underwritten by China — a country that has acquired substantial interests in the mineral wealth of Afghanistan.

Of course, it was not all smooth sailing. Pakistan was worried that the Afghan conflict and its quiet encouragement of jihad had triggered a blowback. Some of the Islamist groups nurtured by the ISI to inflict pain on India had developed autonomous agendas and had even begun targeting the Pakistan military. This threat was partially offset by an unexpected bonanza: India's retreat from its post-26/11 position of 'no talks' until Pakistan completely disavowed terrorism. What is now called the "Mohali spirit" was also premised on the convoluted rationale that the process of normalization would bolster Pakistan's fledgling democracy. However, there is no evidence to suggest that the Pakistani cantonments were worried by this wishful calculation. To them, India's talks with "useful idiots" of the civilian government merely helped Pakistan look more respectable. It was also a great relief to the western powers that valued both countries: India for business and Pakistan for facilitating its exit from Afghanistan.

Abbottabad has nullified this script. It was one thing for Pakistan to be harbouring Mullah Omar in Quetta, but Osama was another matter altogether. Pakistan's perfidy hasn't merely made the US angry; it has been shown to be a sucker. In normal circumstances,

India should have been jubilant and telling the world 'we told you so' — a sentiment echoed by the media and society. Tragically, the latest confirmation of Pakistan's habitually duplicitous conduct has left Manmohan Singh strangely unmoved. He has instead reaffirmed his faith in Pakistan's innate goodness — a gesture of monumental magnanimity that is prone to being misconstrued.

India's wimpish official response to Pakistan's double-dealing isn't likely to generate oodles of gratitude. A beleaguered Pakistan has reacted to its own embarrassment with a heady cocktail of victimhood, nationalism and anti-Americanism. Such an outburst can't be delinked from that country's pet hates. When it comes to India, Pakistan is often loath to even practice *al taqiyya* — so profound is its fear of India's skills of absorption. This may explain Islamabad's calculated over-reaction to notional threats of Indian special operations. For Pakistan, anti-Indianism is the national adhesive.

Pakistan is still unsure of the extent of Western retribution over its sanctuary to Osama. It is banking on a temporary frostiness that will dissipate in the face of the imminent departure from Afghanistan. Pakistan has reposed faith in the two aces it has up its sleeve: its nuclear assets and its firm alliance with China. The West, it believes, will bark but won't dare bite.

In the normal course, India would have been an additional pressure point on Pakistan. Having abandoned that option, India has made itself redundant in the Great Game. Singh may yet get to visit his native village in Pakistan. In craving that privilege, he may also secure India's banishment from Afghanistan and the onward march of China in South Asia.

What after the Jasmine fades?

Ranjan Roy | 20 April 2011

Images of democracy in motion make for intoxicating television. The kid next to the soldier with his tank at Tahrir Square, the exhausted rebel in a Libyan desert and women and children out in Bahrain's Pearl Square. Next stop, democracy, the footage suggests as anchors hurtle to keep pace with the compelling images and churn out the two-minute revolution theory.

The painful truth is that the path to Egypt, Libya, Syria and Yemen emerging as western-style democracies could be torturous and long. And even worse for places like Bahrain and other rich Emirates where civil society has suddenly discovered it has a political mind.

A look at the map of West Asia shows many straight lines drawn across the barren deserts by European powers and civil servants in London to create nations that suited the post-colonial foreign policy needs of colonisers. Little heed was paid to the demographic heterogeneity of the region where an artificial nationality negotiated with the local satrap was imposed on the people. Since then, most countries have lived under autocratic rulers at best and tyrannical at worst. Nasser in Egypt was anti-imperial but not a democrat.

By far the most peaceful and educated civil society in the region is that of Egypt's. But even there, few institutions exist. The heads of state have donned military colours and have exterminated critics and opposition with the help of an all-powerful secret police and perpetrated a regime of fear. Corruption is endemic, made evident by the *baksheesh* culture that permeates all layers of officialdom; courts are arranged to favour the powerful and the upper middle class lives in negotiated comfort with the military. Will all this disappear in one fell swoop? Unlikely. Too many vested interests are entrenched, the biggest among them, the politico-military. Egypt is the best place to make the transition, though. It does have a parliament, a body of legislative rules and a set of laws that the courts can use.

Take the case of Libya, where US intervention looks menacingly like George Bush's regime change war in Iraq. Barack Obama has taken care to broaden Nato involvement but the first few rounds of US attacks muddied the waters and gave Muammar Gaddafi international oxygen to breathe fire against 'American Imperialists'. It's hard to sympathise with Gaddafi, but lifting all forms of control, undemocratic as they may be, will push Libya into violent chaos and reopen tribal faultlines. That the anarchy could be taken advantage of by Islamic extremists isn't unlikely, and dismantling the military overnight will remove a bulwark against mushrooming of terror outfits. The removal of the dictator will create a political vacuum in a country where no political elite barring Gaddafi loyalists has been allowed to flourish. Unlike Syria, where thanks to the Ba'ath Party, the political base is a tad wider, Libya has no second-rung of leadership to fall back on barring tribal leaders and military commanders.

In Syria, where tens of thousands are sitting in for Bashir Assad's ouster, the topography is even more complicated. Despite being overwhelmingly Sunni, Syria is a mosaic of competing faiths and cultures that have been papered over by a socialistic-sounding political system represented by the Ba'ath Party. If the order crumbles, it would expose chasms between the Christians, the Alawis, the Druze, the Ismailiyas and even the Greek Orthodox group. Flux in Syria could also lead to regional complications. The Damascus regime is viewed by many as a cat's paw for Iranian interests. Help to the Hezbollah in Lebanon, locked in a protracted war with Israel, also comes from Damascus and the Assads have a fair amount of clout in how the political structure in the fractured neighbour is arranged. It's insane to predict how things would shape up if Assad falls but violence is a fair certainty.

It's a shame that Bashir Assad didn't loosen up the political system fast enough to prevent this. The breakneck pace at which protests seem to be spreading won't leave him room for gradual change. That apart, the worst fear is that these regimes will fall in the hands of Islamic hardliners. That may or may not happen but the ground is fertile for such an outcome. In countries where regimes have been traditionally repressive, the mosques tend to transform into political arenas where dissidents and critics meet. That apart, the separation of the church and state isn't obligatory even in Islamic democracies.

Lastly, where the legitimacy of the existing ruler is destroyed by a public upsurge and there isn't any clear political succession in the works, clerics could assume leadership roles where none existed for them previously. Human societies crave order, and in situations of strife, clerics promising stability, whatever the terms of such an order are, could gain a mass following.

In Indonesia, when the 1997 Asian economic turmoil eroded dictator Suharto's credibility and finally caused his downfall, the leader of the tolerant Muslim country's largest religious movement, the Nahdnatul Ulama, Abdurrahman Wahid, was nominated as the successor. That Gus Dur, as he was popularly known, was a moderate leader with great respect for the minorities, helped Indonesia complete a transition to a modern parliamentary democracy that subsequently elected liberal leaders like Megawati Sukarnoputri as president. But that's not an outcome that's going to follow if in a vacuum, political space is usurped by religious hardliners with a conservative Islamic vision of civil society.

Wikileaked and scared

Indrani Bagchi | 24 April 2011

WikiLeaks has terrified the Indian government, more than Prakash Karat's barbs during the nuclear deal. All those cables from the US embassy in Delhi, which were serialised in The Hindu shook the system.

Whether its coincidence or a direct result of WikiLeaks, I'm not certain, but an unnatural quiet appears to have descended on India-US relations. For two countries who have publicly sworn undying love to each other through nuclear deals, presidential visits and state dinners, there is a strange torpor in the bilateral space.

This past week, Mitch McConnell, US Republican leader led a five-member high level congressional delegation to India. Not too long ago, this would have generated some news. Not any more. Neither PM Manmohan Singh nor foreign minister SM Krishna met the high level congressional delegation. Krishna had a valid alibi – he was in Nepal. But the PM? McConnell and his group present a unique opportunity to make them speak for India in the Hill.

Insiders in both Washington and New Delhi say both embassies are quite obviously sleeping on the job. The Indian ambassador to Washington, Meera Shankar should be ready to retire and return. And in Delhi, the US embassy has dealt itself out of public discourse on US-India relations. Small wonder that there was little focus on the senators' visit. The senators got to meet national security adviser, Shivshankar Menon, commerce minister Anand Sharma etc during their multi-city tour.

Significantly, McConnell's Democratic counterpart, Harry Reid is in China on a similar mission accompanied by nine senators. China is unconcerned because WikiLeaks may have raged in many parts of the world but not in China. Therefore, Reid will have his most important meeting with Xi Jinping, who is slated to succeed Hu Jintao next year. In previous years, though, congressional delegations have been received at the highest level in the Indian system. The hesitation this time is unusual, sources attributing it to the battering Indian politicians took after WikiLeaks.

Officials, however, rushed to point out that a rash of high level meetings between the US and India are on the cards. Bill Burns, who will now become deputy secretary in the US state department is likely to come for meetings before his confirmation hearings start. The high-tech working group will be meeting here, which acquires importance after India was taken off some categories in the US entities list. Richard Holbrooke's successor, Marc Grossman, will be here at the end of April to talk Afghanistan-Pakistan with India.

The India-US strategic dialogue is slated for July which will see US secretary of state Hillary Clinton visiting here.

A rash of WikiLeaks documents leaked from the US embassy here showed the closeness between US and Indian systems, which has come under a lot of criticism from Left-leaning commentaries. Even the opposition BJP has felt stung by some of the leaks. From Pakistan to Sri Lanka conversations between US diplomats and Indian officials and politicians have been made public coloured by US officials' perceptions of Indians. Surprisingly, despite their public reservations about the US, across the political spectrum, Indian politicians were seen to be more than open with US diplomats.

WikiLeaks has affected all of that, certainly for the foreseeable future.

Oil makes the world go round

Sudeshna Sen | February 22, 2011

This last week, the entire world has been watching in awe as the Arab world erupts. Innumerable commentators who are far more qualified than me are analysing the phenomenon to shreds. I expect this will be one of those historic watersheds that will forever change any discussions about the Middle East, whatever happens in Egypt, Yemen, Libya, Algeria or Bahrain from here on.

Tunisia, which most of us were vaguely aware of as a tourist destination, has suddenly become the centre of world interest. And that brings me to the point I'm trying to make. Where I'm coming from, one of the most fascinating reactions I've got have been from a Pakistani acquaintance here.

"Finally, the Islamic world is in the news for the right reasons, and not because we're all some kind of Terror Ali." For years, we've all been hearing, from every kind of government, social activist and academics that whole spiel about the 'problem of alienated Islamic' youth. It's actually an incredibly hoary old story.

For years, the Arab world has been in the grip of autocratic rulers, propped up by implicit and explicit support from other world governments, just to keep that crucial oil flow coming through.

For years, the poor, the young, the unemployed and the underprivileged, brought up in repressive regimes themselves, have sought succour from the only alternative they find, the likes of al-Qaeda . What those young people in Egypt and Tunisia have done is show up their granddaddies that, yes, there is an alternative to suicide bombing for the alienated, the poor, the young, the huddled masses.

All world governments, including in India, instead of hijacking Egypt's triumph for their own narrow political reasons, should grab this opportunity. And tell their own young and poor that there is a peaceful alternative to suicide bombing and terrorism.

Because the one other thing that has become all too evident is that this is a globalised village. Like epidemics, like financial crises, and everything else, national boundaries are dissolving like never before. The other most fascinating positive lesson is that the best way to get rid of tyrants is simply to outlive them. The eccentric Mr Qaddafi, for instance, may well repress the Libyans now, but well, nature is catching up with him.

In a democracy, there's this illusion that elections can bring about change, but if the subcontinent is an example, all elections give us is one bunch of geriatric incompetents or grandiose General after another. The other big headline story this week is the continuing wrangle between the Indian government and Cairn-Vedanta.

What have I got left to say on that? It drives me to despair when I see sweeping statements about 'national interest' from the oil mandarins. Oh, get real, somebody. It is still absolutely unclear what ONGC's royalty, where ONGC is a commercial partner of Cairn India, has to do with a transfer of parent control between two listed companies on the LSE.

It's also totally ridiculous why this has taken more than six months. Until the recent spate of meetings after the PMO issued a directive, there was absolute stasis for over four months. How on earth, if they didn't conduct negotiations or discussions, did they expect to come to any agreement by end of Jan?

If the petroleum ministry had to refer it to the Cabinet , why wait for eternity? This is absolutely not the time to act all macho about national interest. Find a face-saving excuse, clear the deal and be done with it. Or kiss goodbye to the hope that India will attract even a fraction of that $1 trillion for infrastructure. Before everyone calls me biased, hey, I'm going to have to live with the nuclear fallout from international investors, not the petroleum ministry, so I have every right to be ticked off.

Already, I'm hearing everyday about how much easier LatAm is to invest in. Or Vietnam. Eastern Europe is recovering from recession — and that region has always been a preferred destination. I don't have to tell the readers of this paper that inbound FDI is tanking. International FDI investors don't care about your internal scams, or the gobbledygook about clauses that the Indian government is feeding my colleagues everyday. They look at the final results. The report card is like this.

Cairn UK took the risk of investing in oil exploration in India when nobody would, and they got a favourable deal with their commercial partner ONGC, when nobody knew there was oil in Rajasthan. It's selling its stake in Cairn India to another UK-based company, Vedanta, for which neither needs GoI permission, only the FSA and Sebi's.

Cairn India needs government clearance to transfer the licences. The petroleum ministry wants to change the terms of a commercial agreement signed by ONGC and Cairn India, as a precondition for a transaction between their parents. And then it dithers for six months of complete paralysis.

Would RBI revoke licences for one foreign bank that buys out India operations of another? It wouldn't dream of doing so without serious provocation. What makes the petro min different? That's where it gets all political. If the petroleum ministry wanted to transfer the case to Cabinet, why waste all this time? If they didn't approve of Anil Agarwal, which seems to have been the case originally, they should have found a legal and transparent reason to say so, and scuppered the deal in August last year.

But no, they dither, and posture in public, and get all rhetorical. Now, they're dug in their own hole: neither ONGC nor the petroleum ministry can backtrack from what is fast becoming an untenable position without losing political face, and so have passed hot potato. Don't dither. It spooks people who sink zillions into the arid ground, literally, for 20 years or more. Dithering, it seems will be the lasting epitaph for this government. Sigh.

Corruption per square foot

Abheek Barman | November 16, 2010

What is it with India's property market that makes it the biggest sink of black money in the country? The Adarsh Housing Society scam threatens to topple ministers, politicians and military brass in Maharashtra, but that's unlikely to slow down property transactions in Mumbai, Delhi or anywhere else in the country. Transactions which could involve as much as 60% to 70% of the payment in cash, according to anecdotal evidence.

"Real estate is where most of the cash generated in the economy flows to," says an official in the ministry of finance, who declined to be identified for this article. He should know. In December last year, the ministry compiled the results from income tax investigations across the country: of the relatively modest Rs 4,500 crore it uncovered, nearly half, Rs 2,000 crore was unearthed from real estate. About a quarter of the total was traced to manufacturing and a tenth to bullion and jewellery.

We don't notice it often, but despite its successes in modern technologies and services, India remains a largely cash economy. We pay cash when we pay the cabbie or auto driver, hand over banknotes to the family help and despite the growth of organized retail, do most of our essential shopping at the local *kirana* store where the gentleman has a sign that reads, "In god we trust, rest only cash."

One such store we visited claimed to service 300 households in the neighbourhood, supplying everything from soaps and shampoos to cooking oil, flour, butter, biscuits and even cleaners and plastic utensils. The owner refused to talk about his sales or earnings, but the math isn't hard to do. Let's say a household spends Rs 15,000 every month on essentials. Then the take for this store would be Rs 45 lakh every month.

Retail margins vary widely, from as little as 5% for soaps and shampoos to as high as 50% to 100% for foods and baltis, but an average margin of say, a third, would leave the store owner with a profit of Rs 15 lakh a month. That's Rs 1.8 crore a year. From one corner store in south Delhi. And it's all cash.

Every time you see a truck on the road, chances are high that the trucker's been paid in cash. An average 9 tonne truck charges about Rs 25,000 for a full load for a Delhi-Mumbai run, and can do about 100 such runs in a year, so that's Rs 25 lakh per truck in a year, mostly cash, because India's trucking industry is heavily fragmented: of the 5.2 million trucks on the road today, over 4 million are run by people who own 10 trucks or less.

The taxman's survey found manufacturing generating a lot of cash. That's surprising because it should be relatively easy to measure – and tax – what comes out of factories. Not quite so, explains the finance ministry official. "In the past when we had excise inspectors physically present at excise gates, most factories had a second gate to take untaxed output to the market," he says, "VAT was supposed to change all that, but people have found ways around that too."

If you drive a car, I'll tax the street
If you try to sit, I'll tax your seat
If you get too cold I'll tax the heat
If you take a walk, I'll tax your feet
Taxman!
Cos I'm the taxman, yeah I'm the taxman
(Taxman, lyrics by George Harrison)

It's hard to tell whether Indira Gandhi was inspired by the Beatles, but since the 1970s, when she hiked top income tax rates to 90%-plus, well heeled Indians have played cat and mouse with the taxman with gusto. In the early 2000s, economist Arun Kumar reckoned that about half of India's wealth was stashed away as black money: in a trillion dollar economy, that's about $500 billion.

Some of this money is salted away overseas. A few years ago, a Ford Foundation sponsored study by think tank Global Financial Integrity (GFI) found that Indians had salted away $23 to $31 billion dollars overseas in the year 2006, ranking it fifth after China, Saudi Arabia, Mexico and Russia. If you take the oil producers out of the list, India comes second after China in taking money out of the country illegally.

India's economy has grown since then and it's safe to assume so has the volume of funds salted away overseas. But even if you double the outflows to $50 billion, there's still another $450 billion sloshing around in the country. You can't eat two breakfasts a day, you can't buy too many expensive cars with cash, so what are the best places to park cash? Bullion of course, but real estate is right on top.

"It's out there, you don't need to hide it, it can't be stolen and the best thing, it doesn't have a price sticker on it telling the government how much you paid for it," explains the head of a Delhi-based real estate brokerage that does deals for high networth clients, who requested anonymity.

It's not that governments haven't tried to keep tabs on — and tax — property. For several years, the Delhi government has assigned something called 'circle rates' — the minimum prices at which property can be traded in the city. It recently hiked these rates, in some areas even doubling them to Rs 125,000 per square metre. That narrowed, but hasn't closed the gap between the official and market rates. For example, the highest circle rate could still be as low as a fifth to a quarter of what you'd actually pay in these areas.

"The market is changing for the better," says the real estate brokerage head, "more professionals are entering the market, forcing builders to accept cheque payments, forcing the cash component down." Even then, he reckons that most secondary transactions have a cash component between 40% and 50%. The cash market is fickle, he explains. In many cases it depends on the background of the seller and how much he's paid in cash.

"Businessmen have more cash than professionals. And if someone's paid 70% in cash to buy, he'll want the same when he's selling," shrugs the broker, "History matters, you know."

Invest, as crude prices soar

TK Arun | March 10, 2011

Crude prices are rising and are likely to remain high for quite some time, even after the democratic upsurge in the Arab countries subsides — victorious, we hope, rather than vanquished. India needs to respond proactively to the rising prices, through short and medium-term steps. Most of them entail fresh investment, and will boost growth in a relatively climate-benign fashion.

As this newspaper's editorial argued earlier this week, one short-term measure that can be explored is swapping food for oil. India has foodgrain stocks in excess of the buffer-stocking norm while most oil-exporting countries import grain, also rising in price. India's excess stocks tend to rot on account of poor storage. Instead, India should think of trading this grain for oil. The stability this brings to a portion, at least, of the country's oil imports would tend to reduce price volatility for the rest of the demand as well.

We must commence blending ethanol into petrol. It has already begun in a small way, but the point is to reduce the consumption of petrol by 10%, not create yet more grist for semiotic analysis. This will mean setting up new sugar mills and ethanol plants, and growing more cane, preferably in water-rich Bihar rather than as expansion in arid Maharashtra, where the crop grows sucking up subsidy by the acre-foot.

India must build up oil stocks. Is this the right time to begin building stocks, when prices are high? Certainly, it would be stupid to buy when prices spike, but depending on our ability to negotiate prices close to the trend, we should buy oil to build stocks, rather than wait for prices to fall. These stocks would dampen future volatility. The developed countries have built up stocks, while in India, we have only talked about it, for years.

This is the easy bit. The tough part is raising retail oil prices, or more specifically, decontrolling them. There is no better way to conserve energy than to price in its full cost. Subsidising fuel encourages profligate consumption, while the entire drive of policy should be to minimise consumption by boosting efficiency, reducing usage and resort to substitution wherever possible. And raising diesel prices is the big-ticket reform, because diesel accounts for the bulk of petrofuel consumption.

But it is not enough to allow diesel prices to rise. A lot of diesel use is unresponsive to price. If goods have to be hauled by road, they will be hauled by trucks, regardless of the cost of diesel. Of course, higher diesel prices would encourage people to opt for vehicles with greater fuel-efficiency, but this saving is not enough.

Coastal shipping, inland waterways, rail and modern blimps — why not? — offer far greater scope for energy saving. But these call for massive investment.

It is criminal for the government to hold investment in rail hostage to coalition compulsions. We need massive investment in new lines, doubling and renewal of existing tracks, computerised signalling, new rolling stock and electrification.

Diversion of traffic from road to rail would save energy and also switch fuel from diesel to coal and gas. Coal mining and value addition must cease to be a state monopoly and opened up to private enterprise and competition. Natural gas prices have effectively got delinked from crude prices, thanks to the doubling of global gas reserves that took place between 2008 and 2009, from 400 trillion cu ft to 800 trillion cu ft, essentially due to new capability to tap into shale gas. India is yet to take advantage of this delinking, having entered into long-term contracts to import liquefied natural gas (LNG) at prices linked to crude prices. The country now needs to invest in new LNG terminals and pipeline networks to take advantage of low-cost natural gas available. Gas availability can quickly yield new power-generation capacity with superior thermal efficiency and short gestation periods. This presupposes political will to render power commercially viable through the simple expedient of ending political patronage of power theft. But the biggest reform of all would be new town planning. In city after city, people waste up to three hours in snarled traffic everyday, commuting to and from work. In the process, they guzzle fuel, spew out pollution and build up plaque in their coronary arteries. Let us have compact, vertical towns, residential blocks abutting office buildings, public transport running on electric motors or natural gas, green parks and playgrounds that produce future Olympics medal winners.

India will need more than 20,000 sq km of new urban land to accommodate the workforce that will drive industry and services to deliver sustained 9%-plus growth for the economy. Let us invest to make them less vulnerable to crude price volatility than our present slum infestations are.

India has to act, in the face of rising crude prices, to contain the impact on the economy. Short-term measures apart, a cogent response calls for large-scale investment. Political courage and imagination constrain our response, rather than funds.

In trust deficit too, China races ahead of India

Abheek Barman | April 13, 2011

Those of us who suffer from China-envy — the debilitating feeling that the Chinese are ahead of us in everything they do, should think about this. The average Chinese trusts her government even less than we trust ours.

Is that possible, after CWG, Adarsh and Andimuthu Raja? It is. About a fortnight ago, there were fears that radiation from Fukushima could leak into seawater, and eventually salt. This sent thousands to Chinese rushing to grocery stores. They cleaned out entire shops of all the packaged salt in store. This triggered fears of a salt shortage in coastal China.

The government insisted the fears were baseless, as indeed they proved to be, but people took their neighbours' whispers more seriously than the word from Beijing.

Something even more serious is happening from last week. Folks across China have cleared shop shelves of soaps, detergents and shampoo. For the last week or so, media has said that the four companies that dominate this business, including Unilever and P&G and two Chinese entities, will hike prices of soaps and shampoos between 5% and 15%.

None of these four companies has actually hiked rates, nor spoken about the timing of price hikes. Beijing insists that interest rate hikes and other measures will soon cool prices. Nevertheless, people have panicked.

Yes, inflation is high in China, but India has also gone through a period of gut-wrenching price spikes. Yet, we do not see crowds stampeding through vegetable markets, or cleaning out store shelves before Haldiram makes its *bhujia* costlier. The only panic buying you're likely to see is at the local *theka*, the evening before the next dry day.

In newsrooms, it used to be said that you couldn't trust news out of China till Beijing denied it. Today, most Chinese seem to believe this. They don't trust their government and if the mandarins say something, they're betting that exactly the opposite is true.

Here, it's different. To most things *sarkari*, the Indian responds with a cynical shrug. The exception is the government calendar of dry days, which are many in a year. That, we treat with all the seriousness it deserves.

Is Sachin the greatest of all? The debate rages on

Bobilli Vijay Kumar | 26 December 2010

So, is Sachin Tendulkar the greatest sportsperson ever? The question, raised by TOI on Friday, has triggered a furious debate in blogosphere: the answers, expectedly, have ranged from emphatic yeses to shocked nos.

Yes, even today, there are many Sachin sceptics: Imran Khan, for one, has always maintained that Inzamam was much, much more talented; those who have seen Lara in flow swear by his exquisiteness and flourish; the Aussies, of course, can't see beyond Ponting, even if he is currently batting like Boycott's grandma.

To understand the Sachin myth, therefore, one has to go back to the beginning: numbers, as strange as it may seem now, were never part of his original USP; it was his quiet confidence and divine strokeplay.

He could conjure shots out of even unplayable deliveries, leaving both the bowler and the spectator gaping in awe. During those early days, there were no calm moments at the crease; there only used to be a buzz, an excitement from the time he walked in till he left for the day, falling to some other audacious hit. If you wanted to see serenity, you simply turned towards the batsman at the other end.

The sceptics argue that Donald, at his fiercest, had Sachin's measure; that McGrath could outwit him anytime, anywhere; that Akram too was far too cunning for him. Intriguingly, he struggled against ordinary new spinners, almost like a kid would labour with a foreign name.

So, forget being the greatest sportsperson, can he even be called the greatest batsman of all time? The answer to that is simple: Bradman is, no doubt, the original run-machine. But his legacy was built around two numbers: 29 centuries and 99.94 average in Tests. For a long time, 29 seemed like Mount Everest: out there, but impossible to scale. Finally, in the early 80s, Gavaskar conquered it. Since then, seven batsmen have gone past Bradman. Once the peak was conquered, it didn't invoke any fear.

The 99.94, however, is another matter: like the sun, it shall probably remain forever, even after everything else has been reduced to dust. Batsmen, therefore, needed to attack his legend from another angle, another prism. Sachin, in his own way, has done that with his record-breaking appetite and longevity. He changed with the times, according to the needs of his body, the schemes of the opposition, the pitches around him and even the players within his own team. Almost each time, he proved to be one step ahead of the hurdle, amassing runs and hundreds.

Yet, the X-factor was always elusive; that something special to add the crown to his aura was still missing. It eventually came last week, when he slammed his 50th Test century; he had finally equalled the Don. No eyebrows shot up when the "greatest" question propped up again; even the Aussies grudgingly handed over the mantle.

Sachin, though, is not yet done. He wants to surpass the Don and there is only one way to do it: a complete century, a full 100. Well, he just needs four more hundreds for that; it would be perfect if he can take his 46 ODI tons up. But any four will do. After that, there won't be a single sceptic.

On to the big question then: how does Sachin rank before the Peles, the Federers, the Woods, the Alis, generally acknowledged as the very best in their respective sports? Well, does Sachin become less greater because cricket is played by very few countries, and even fewer when it comes to Test cricket? Surely not.

An important test of greatness is the impact a player has on the game, and the society. For those who remember, when Sachin came along India was in a flux, just about beginning its march towards superpowerdom; it was still like a baby, taking its first few steps and every little progress and achievement was hailed as path-breaking. Life was not yet as exciting and promising as it is now and smiles were few and far between.

Tendulkar was the first beacon around that time, and cricket the only salve for a country in pain. Every time he came out to bat, India came to a standstill. All the worries of the daily grind, the tensions between the various communities — particularly after the Babri Masjid fallout — were forgotten. The country smiled when he scored runs; it plunged into gloom when he got out.

Cricket had already become the number one sport in the country; but India was still not a dominant team: the Big Five were yet to forge their amazing partnership. So, the country got its little pleasures from individual conquests, from Sachin's exploits primarily.

Tendulkar passes all tests with equal ease; his legend, like everything mortal, will only rise when he stops playing. Only a long time after that, people will realize how extraordinary his achievements really were, how great he really is.

Proud to be an Indian

Saibal Bose | 03 April 2011

Did you on Saturday night, feel a certain level of euphoria that you have never experienced before?

Did you rush out into the street to celebrate, like millions of Indians, as soon as Mahendra Singh Dhoni smashed that historic six? Raise your arms in a spontaneous expression of ecstasy; dancing, screaming and celebrating like never before? Did you go crazy with joy, letting your hair down in the dead of the night in a devil-may-care manner, climbing on rooftops, car-tops and on bikes, waving the Tricolour and soaking in the greatest moment of your life? Spraying colours that you had saved from Holi and bursting more crackers than you would at Diwali?

When Yuvraj Singh, wrapped in an Indian flag, cried after banishing a few demons, did you have to fight back your tears too? Were you ready to scream with Harbhajan Singh, jump with Virat Kohli, run with R Ashwin, sway with Virender Sehwag...? Or were you just stone-faced, like Dhoni, rubbing the eyes occasionally to betray your emotions? Did you put a hand on your heart like Amir Khan, not quite believing what you had just witnessed; kept smiling from ear to ear like Rajnikanth in blue India colours; shook a million hands like Rahul Gandhi; sang the song of victory with thousands like Preity Zinta? Did you do all that and much more?

When a legend called Sachin Tendulkar was carried by his mates on a trip around the Wankhede ground, did a lump suddenly appear in your throat? Were you also saying over and over again that this one is for Sachin, who has carried India's hopes for 21 years and keeps doing so? Did you feel the urge to barge into the Team India celebrations, give Sachin a thump on his back and say: you deserve it the most? You have been a true champion and without you, this would not have been possible. Were you dreaming of being in Kohli's shoes, with Sachin perched on your shoulders and the Flag fluttering in his hands?

Were you wanting to walk up to Kapil's Devils and telling them that they were no longer alone at the top? That they were very good, but this bunch is perhaps better, maybe the best cricket team that India has produced? Were you eager to thank the Gavaskars, Binnys and Amarnaths for the great memories that they have given us for 28 years and telling them that now, it is time for some new ones? That the wait has been worth it? Did you want to look up Sourav Ganguly and say: Hey Dada, you almost took us to the pinnacle in 2003. The defeat to Australia hurt. Not any longer, a new beginning has been made: the beginning of a new era.

On Saturday night, were you proud to be an Indian?

Why was Summer of 83 sweeter?

Raja Bose | 03 April 2011

It was a balmy June night. The mercury was rising, so was the excitement. Will we do the impossible? Will we see history in the making?

I wondered if people felt the same minutes before Jawaharlal Nehru unfurled the Indian flag for the first time to begin India's tryst with destiny. It definitely was a defining moment on the night of June 25, 1983. When India became the world champions in cricket, despite running the risk of sounding blasphemous, I think it overshadowed the stroke of midnight moment of August 14, 1947.

Cut to April 2, 2011. Yet another night of excitement, of history being written. While Indian captain Mahendra Singh Dhoni took India to a great victory, I was struck by a strange feeling — I was not getting as excited as I should have been.

My heart wasn't beating as fast. My palms weren't sweaty. I wasn't pacing up and down the room. I didn't even have my lucky handkerchief in my hand, something I do every time I wanted India to win, every time I took an examination.

I must admit it did bother me that I wasn't super excited. I could already hear the fire-crackers outside my house. My daughter was jumping in joy with every big hit. After the win, I drove with my family across Chandigarh, joined in the revelry. But ... there was something amiss.

Probably it's the age. I was a starry-eyed 16-year-old then. I am 44 now. Was it the exuberance of youth that made witnessing history so much sweeter? That goes reason one.

Probably it was the unexpected nature of the 1983 win that made it so exciting. India was nowhere in the previous two World Cups in 1975 and 1979. We had beaten the West Indies in one game in the 1983 Cup. Kapil Dev had scored that epoch-making 175 against Zimbabwe on the road to the final.

But, nobody believed we could be on the top of the world. Not even when Kapil did the unthinkable again with that great athletic catch to dismiss Viv Richards. It was only when West Indian wickets kept falling that the feeling began to sink in. Can we? Yes, we can. Will we just lose it? Maybe, we can!

It's human nature. When you get something you never expected, it tastes much, much sweeter. This time, we all knew, India had the strength, and the team, to win the cup. Twenty-eight years ago, a friend was willing to bet with Rs 1,000 against an India win (and mind you, we were in high school then and that was one heck of an amount). On the eve of the 2011 World Cup final, the stakes were heavily loaded in favour of India.

And, when Dhoni hit the winning stroke, I wanted to see it again, and again. And, television showed it to me again, and yet again. Not just the whole of last night, I saw it this morning too.

Can you beat this? I watched India's win over the West Indies in the 1983 final six months after that great day, when I could lay my hands on a VHS video. Unbelievable, right? But that was India, almost a decade before our economy opened up. Jamshedour, the town I grew up in, did not even have a television station till 1984!

I savoured the video as much as I could, playing it over and over again before it was time to return the video cassette to the neighbourhood video store. I did not even mind the scratches and the stars caused by people before me playing it so many times over, rewinding those great moments to keep them recorded in memory for posterity.

But can you escape a Dhoni or Yuvraj today? If they are not playing a Test, an ODI, a T20 or IPL, they are all around you 24x7, selling sports shoes, cars, mobile phones, energy capsules and hair oil.

The bombardment of their faces does take the charm away. If Dhoni isn't directing his bowlers on the ground, he is selling you apps. The aura of a ravishing Sandip Patil among our female friends and the ooh and aahs they broke into every time the dashing Roger Binny went on to bowl, was stuff of jealous nights for us guys.

There is no disputing that the post-83 generation loved every moment of the match, enjoyed every second of the frenzied post-match celebrations out on the streets. But, could it have been a tad better without the commercialization of our cricketing heroes?

A free market is as inevitable as an idea whose time has come, but could have Dhoni been a bigger star, a more respected cricketer had he not peddled aerated drinks for us all through day and night?

One could argue that it's a case of sour grapes. Apart from that famous Kapil *da jawab nahin* and Gavaskar modelling for a suiting firm (apart from Sandip Patil and Syed Kirmani acting in a flop Bollywood flick), hardly any cricketing star went the commercial way.

What's wrong in modelling and making money when you are winning the World Cup too? Nothing. But, in our daily, humdrum lives, we need to look up high.

And, there are gods and there are demi-gods. The choice is clear.

If 1983 was history, 2011 is a footnote in bold. If 1983 was a romance, 2011 is happily ever after.

Saina: the golden girl with nerves of steel

Bobilli Vijay Kumar | 16 October 2010

Saina Nehwal is rarely in a hurry on the badminton court; the only time she seems to be restless or edgy is when she is ready to serve. Even before her opponent has gathered her wits, or breath, she is poised with shuttle and racquet.

But that's not because of any tingling in the nerves or rattling in the mind: her heart is steady and quickly back to is normal beating rate; her eyes are cool and her face is calm as a blank canvas.

Indeed, for the most part, she is inscrutable and in control of her inner demons; you can see a flicker of emotion only when she wins a point: her palm folds into a wrist and she pumps it vigorously, once, twice, thrice. Her scream cuts through the packed stadium but quickly merges with the roars of appreciation.

Within a second, the mask is back on her face, and she is ready to serve.

Saina's eagerness to start quickly is, however, not a fetish: It is a well thought out strategy; it is the one clear sign of, both, confidence and superiority. She has worked so hard on her fitness and stamina that she rarely, if ever, loses on the fatigue front; indeed, she has packed so much energy in her reservoirs that even Maruti or Hero Honda would be envious.

One saw her battle it out in the Commonwealth Games final, and came back with even more admiration. Her opponent, Malaysia's Wong Mew Choo, had come well prepared. She was swifter in her court coverage, equally adept at net-play and had a powerful and deceptive smash too.

She stayed ahead, for the most part, and seemed to be well in command over the match; indeed, she was even on the brink of winning the championship too, at match point. Sadly, she disintegrated at that moment; she didn't dare look Saina in the eye, which was the cue the Indian was waiting for her.

She moved in for the kill.

Saina, though, had one thing going for her: experience. Apart from confidence, crowd support and also that reservoir to tap from, that is. In the opener, she employed a waiting game, prolonging the rallies and tiring her opponent; in the second, she unveiled her attacking repertoire, mixing drop shots with cross-court hits and body smashes; in the decider, she literally toyed with Wong, teasing her and making her run around like an errand girl.

It was a well calculated ploy, which presumably, is part of her game-plan against higher-ranked players; in all her solidity, however, she also has a gambler's instinct: she is not afraid of taking her chances on the backline when the high tosses can just be out, or excruciatingly on the line. She refuses to give in at the net, either, making the dribble tighter and shorter.

On both counts, she won as many points as she lost, but that didn't deter her. She simply smiled and was ready for the next gamble.

We have in her a champion who has been prepared like a thoroughbred; she follows mentor Gopichand's punishing schedule without a grimace or complaint. She has a goal in her life; and it is tougher than scaling the Chinese Wall all by oneself, without even any climbing equipment.

The feisty Khel Ratna, winner of Super Series titles, though, is not afraid: she realizes that the summit is near but very, very difficult to conquer; but she is in no hurry: at 20, she has age on her side and confidence in her bag. It is just a question of time now.

Reluctant lover

Jug Suraiya | 24 March 2011

Fearful of loss, I've always been a reluctant lover. And after the last time, Bunny and I said 'Never again'. Not having children, we can't imagine the devastation the loss of a child must cause to parents. But the death of Brindle — the street dog who adopted us 13 years ago — was enough. No more dogs, no more loving them. The pain of loss made love too costly, unaffordable.

Get another dog, friends advised. No way. In any case, we hadn't got Brindle, she'd got us. Then — uncannily, on the same day that Brindle died — another dog, helpless, hungry and homeless, came into our lives.

We called her Mili, as in someone met or found. We'll look after her, we said. But we're not going to repeat the mistake of loving her, we agreed, proud of our cautious cunning.

Bunny was the first to succumb, cradling Mili's head in her lap, worrying whether Mili was eating enough, feeling secure enough. I resisted as long as I could, then gave up. And in giving up I learnt a little, a very little, about that odd thing that for want of another word we call love.

There are many varieties of it. There's romantic love, all red hearts and roses and whispered endearments. There's the love of parents for children, and children for parents. There's love of friends, and of one's country. For many, there is love of God, and the love we'd like to think She has for us. And then there's the love that some of us have for our animal companions (I hate the term pets; I am not sentimental about animals).

All these very different kinds of love seem to have one thing in common. And that's the odd, the funny part of it: love is the only thing in the world that the more of it you give away the more of it you seem to have. It's like exercise. The more you exercise the greater the stamina and endurance you develop to do even more exercise.

Love is often thought of as a warm, fuzzy, cuddly feeling, like a teddy bear or a stuffed doll. A comfy and cosy security blanket. Love can be all of that. But it can, and it very often is, the very opposite of something soft and comfortable and comforting. It can be hard, and unyielding, and demanding of attention, like a stone in your shoe, or grit in your eye. It intrudes into your world, into your life, into your way of seeing things, and it does so without even the courtesy of asking you your permission to do so. Love is a hostile take-over bid. It takes you over whether you like it or not. And in doing so, it gives you more than you ever had before, or ever imagined or dreamt that you could have.

Love takes your world, your way of looking at things — your hopes and your fears, your needs and desires and aspirations — and doubles, and then doubles it again, by multiplying your world with the world of the one you love, whoever or whatever that loved one may be: spouse, child, parent, country, God. Or, in my case, a street dog who found me by pure chance.

In that it is often determined by chance — if you had chanced to be born in Pakistan instead of India, you'd have loved Pakistan instead of India, rooted for Pakistan instead of India in the World Cup — love is like a lottery. And like a lottery it can suddenly and without warning enrich you unmeasurably by enlarging your world to accommodate the world of your loved one.

I scan the morning headlines of natural and man-made disasters, of the spreading virus of violence and hatred between people and people, nation and nation. What can possibly be the answer to all this, if answer at all there is? Can it be a single, ridiculous sounding four-letter word called love? How utterly absurd.

Mili thumps her tail on the carpet. Of course it is, the tail agrees. Come scratch me behind my ear, the tail demands. No longer reluctant lover, I bend down and oblige.

Lips don't lie: The Royal kiss Kate and William shared!

Vinita Dawra Nangia | 02 May 2011

As kisses go, this one was no sizzler. It was a happy, somewhat embarrassed quick peck, rather than a passionate smooch that scorches and simmers. The second attempt to make up for the blink-and-you-have-missed-it kiss wasn't any better, with the patrons looking more amused than bemused as they executed another butterfly flutter.

In fact, nourished as we are on a diet of passionate smooches and 22-kisses-a-movie promises, the lip-lock between Prince William and his bride, the newly anointed Duchess of Cambridge Kate Middleton, was a royal disappointment! Admittedly the pressure to perform on the two was immense, with two billion around the world gathered to witness their first snog as a royal couple. What else did you expect of the British, snickered a colleague. They are so cold they are known to make love with their socks on! But still, you do expect much more from a couple who has had almost a decade to perfect the art!

The saving grace was that in admirable contrast to Prince Charles's stiff cold-lipped greeting of his shy bride Princess Diana 30 years ago, son William was warmer and more human. Still, a somewhat sad-looking, shy Di arching her graceful long neck to reach for Charles's reluctant royal lips is a far more picture-worthy and touching moment than the coming together of the new royals who, after all, looked like any other young couple in love!

However, William's kiss was no display of British coldness, but of royal decorum. Stepping back from the first kiss, delivered with his hands clasped together tellingly in front of him, William is supposed to have murmured "I love you" to his bride. Or so say lip readers, the latest tool of paparazzi. The lascivious crowd exhorted, "More, more, we want more...kiss again!" Lip readers decipher the prince's next words thus, "'Let's give them another one. I love you. One more kiss, one more kiss, okay." And the couple leaned in to yet another 'lip-sealed' sedate peck. But this time they couldn't conceal the amusement in their eyes or the happy smile on their lips. Kate giggled, William grinned.

The crowd shouted in ecstasy as the storybook walk of 'one of them' from commoner to princess was sealed with a kiss, so what if it was a sealed-lip kiss!

The tightly pursed mouths and conscious restraint clearly signified the beginning of a more responsible relationship, one that takes into account the burden of responsibility that future monarchy imposes on young William and Kate. No more can they cavort in public. Perhaps that is why the young couple took nine years to formalise their relationship; the only thing that changes with the vows is that their embraces and public dalliances are henceforth subject to public approval or disapproval as behaviour befitting the future king and queen. In fact, the couple didn't seal their wedding with a kiss at Westminster Abbey as the Church of England forbids it in holy sites. With this wedding, Diana's son has formally and consciously stepped into the royal frame set up for him since birth.

Back in 1981, when the crowds clamoured for a Charles and Diana kiss on the balcony after they married, Charles reportedly murmured to Di, "I am not going to do that caper. They are trying to get us to kiss." And she is supposed to have responded, "Well, how about it?" Their body language showed a miserable-looking Charles's extreme reluctance, portending a disastrous marriage.

The body language of young William and Kate was diametrically opposite. Happy, totally in love, shy, exchanging loving glances and sharing a clear connect — body experts talk of their 'total confidence' and how they looked into each other's eyes while taking their vows. The young couple was regally composed with an irrepressible happiness shining through. Just like the kiss that will, for a long time to come, be a defining image of their wedding day.

Be good in what you do — it'll work

Kingshuk Mukherji | 29 April 2011

I have a grouse against some science and mathematics teachers. More often than not, they've left me cold with a sense of foreboding. I am dead against typecasting people. But feel compelled to write this because I suffered at the hands of some teachers who at the outset talked of the difficulties and not of joy.

Only the other day, I met a couple of senior mathematic teachers and was mighty relieved I don't have to sit in their class. These gentlemen teach at schools and also coach kids for the big IIT exam and other engineering entrance tests that every kid in town wants to crack.

One of them held out this particularly dark prospect. "Practice, practice, practice. The key lies in practice," his voice rang out — eyebrows corrugated, not a trace of a smile on his face as he almost threatened to put kids through a wringer to make them IIT-ready.

"Study 12-14 hours a day from day one and you won't have problems. Don't do that and you're in serious trouble," he droned. A clutch of students sitting in a firing squad straight line heard him in silence — eyes wide shut, jaws dropping.

He made it very clear that his drill was for the IIT exams. The plus 2 syllabus wasn't his bother. "Do all that at home." What about the joy of learning? Sorry, you've got the wrong address.

Frankly, I can't blame this guy for being the way he is. He's out in the market and has a success potion to sell. Given the crowd of enthusiastic young faces at his doorsteps, he must be mighty good at stuffing his smart recipe down eager gullets.

"Classes begin at 6.30am and end at 9.30am, that's when I get ready for work. Teaching is a passion and I love it when my students leap over the IIT hurdle...It's the toughest test to clear and needs dedication," he says. The teacher's magic tuitions come at a pretty steep price and he cautions: "Come to me only if you mean business. Don't waste your parents' money."

Numbed by the master's sternness, I stepped out on the pavement and gulped in the evening air. Many years ago, an equally stern mathematics teacher had humiliated me and shut me out from learning the numbers saying: "Go. Ask your parents to buy you a watermelon. You are good for pulling rickshaws." This was after I had scored a zero in a class test.

He had left me with a steely resolve to succeed despite not knowing how to put two and two together. Later, when I picked up arts, they told me I was no good and had taken the girlie-girlie way. Science was the man thing. Big guys with brains became engineers and doctors. Commerce was just another option. BComs are *buddhi com* (dimwit), they scoffed. Never mind if CAs and finance wizards commanded the big pay packets in the jobs bazaar.

No disrespect meant, but I never could see wisdom in cramming my head off and believing nothing else exists just for an examination, which might be as tough to crack as IIT. Also, I didn't see sense in seeing non-IIT, non-science, non-mathematics graduates as lesser mortals short on grey matter.

The moot lesson life taught me was that doing anything well was difficult. To be among the best anywhere needs sincerity and dedication. A good BA is just as valued as a good BTech or an excellent MBBS. You are a dud if you have a medical degree and say I don't know much about the heart. It wasn't important, wasn't expecting questions from that chapter, so I skipped it. Haven't we met engineers who get flummoxed when asked to fix a broken fuse?

'Value for money' Premji

Kingshuk Nag | 03 December 2010

When I moved to Bangalore in the beginning of 1998, Azim Pemji and Wipro were already well-known names there. In Delhi, from where I moved, nobody except those from fields related to computers had heard of Wipro, much less Azim Premji. Although Wipro was well regarded, stories current in Bangalore at that time about Azim Premji related to his 'careful about money' habits. Azim Premji flew economy class and there was this tale about him taking an auto from the airport after disembarking from a flight and not finding his car. Everybody in Bangalore knew that he was a rich guy who was extremely simple and would do things such as borrowing magazines from the staff periodical pool with the promise of returning them later. He was also known as the discerning boss who, among other things, would look at the shoes of his employees to figure out whether they were polished or not! But otherwise, Premji was known to be shy and reticent, not very accessible and would avoid parties and conferences.

My work brought me in touch with Premji very soon and I realised that contrary to the first impression, he was very forthright when pressed about any issue. One day I quizzed him about the various part-time directors on the board of his company. "Why are they there? Do they serve any purpose or say yes to whatever you say and are happy to collect their fees? Who is this Hamir Vissanji on your board?" I asked him. "Oh, he, what should I say, he is like a bania. He comes 2-3 days before each board meeting and pores through the account books and asks my finance managers tough questions about all expenditures. He is very useful in controlling costs." He had similar answers about the utility of other directors who included former Hindustan Lever chairman Ashok Ganguly and international marketing guru Jagdish Sheth from Emery University.

If 'value for money' was a guiding principle of Premji's life, so was his practical nature. It was not unusual for Premji to land up at the premises of customers for a sales pitch for his computers. If a good order could be bagged – and this could be anywhere in India – Premji disregarded his high status and became a salesman. I asked him about this, pointing out that most big honchos would refuse to do anything like this. Premji replied: "My principle in life is simple. If I have got work with you I come to you, if you have got work with me, you come. It is in my interest to sell computers, so I go."

It was in 1999 I think that I chanced upon some authentic data about the shareholding structure of Wipro. Till then this was a well-kept secret. Using the data I found that Premji's wealth was more than a billion dollars. This made him the richest man in India at that time. (According to present computations, Premji is the third richest Indian with a wealth of $ 18 billion.) The news when broken in our newspaper had its own impact and was soon picked up by other newspapers and magazines. Premji started moving up the publicity stakes and a certain kind of halo started surrounding him. All this coincided with the software boom naturally adding to his lustre. Though Azim Premji never expressed this openly, the feeling I got was that he felt that rival Infosys was always ahead of his company in the publicity sweepstakes and he could not fathom why this was so. Who would tell him that N R Narayanamurthy, the boss of Infosys picked his own phone and his deputy Nandan Nilekani could be found in social gatherings that made him very accessible? Premji in contrast was largely unavailable to the media and would give nightmares to his PR managers.

Premji's philosophy in life however did not change after he was discovered to be the richest Indian. One evening, Premji learnt that we were doing a story somewhat adverse to him. In those days cellphones were not that common and at least I did not possess one. By the time Premji was able to trace me it was already past 10pm. He wanted to come and meet me. I told him that it was late and that I was in the coffee shop of Hotel Oberoi with a friend. Imagine my surprise when Premji landed up at the hotel at around 11pm, his PR managers in tow, just to explain his side of the story to me.

Sometimes Premji gave answers to questions that really stumped you. One of his top executives had left him and there was a whiff of a discordant note in the air. I asked Premji: "You kicked him out or he kicked you and went away?" Premji replied: "That guy has got used to the luxury of living in India and has become lazy ... I asked him to go to the US and expand Wipro's business there, but he refused. Naturally, here he has 10 servants, there he won't have even one. So we had to part ways."

In those days, Premji also used to espouse a revolutionary idea. "The dominant shareholder of the company need not be the person who holds managerial control of the company. It is not necessary that my son succeeds me in this company. As the dominant shareholder he can enjoy the profits, but if he is not the best manager around why should he be the managing director of the company?" he used to say (or something like this). Ten years later I believe that his son is working in Wipro. May be Premji has realised that sonny is a good manager after all. The son, I understand, was trained in GE in the US. This is a company whose practices had influenced Azim Premji a great deal and he used to make no bones about stating so in those days.

Though he had grown up in Bombay, Premji with his practical approach and "value for money approach" was Gujarati at heart. I do not know whether he realises this. His ancestors came from Kutch. Premji, however, could not speak very good Gujarati or Kutchi. He told me how he had gone to see Dhirubhai Ambani once. Finding another Gujarati, Dhirubhai, whose voice had started slurring after a stroke, started talking to Azimbhai in colloquial Gujarati. Premji could not understand a thing, but unwilling to show his ignorance started nodding at everything that Dhirubhai said.

Gujaratis and Kutchis consider Bombay to be the capital of Gujarat and love the city. So did Premji till the 1992 riots shook him. He decided to move out and make the garden city of Bangalore his home. Well Bombay or Mumbai's loss has been Bangalore's gain. A large part of the $2 billion (Rs 8850 crore) charity that Azim Premji made a few days ago will go towards funding a private university in Bangalore. Had he stayed back in Mumbai probably the private university would have come up in the Mumbai area. But one thing is certain: Premji will make sure that the money that he has donated is spent wisely.

Buri nazar waley, terey muh par chasma

Kannan Somasundaram | 09 December 2010

The kindest compliment anybody could give my father was, "He looks fine". It would hearten me so much that I would always repay the thought, adding tributes about the sprightliness and rowdy cheer of the compliment-giver's parents. That privilege to praise, however, was revoked the day my father died.

Now, some people I know parse my comment on good health of their kin for bitterness, sadness, and that dreadful Indian curse: *buri nazar.* For instance, the 89-year-old father of a relative will be whistling his way through the daily routine of 100 single-handed press-ups, but his son – charged with keeping count – will look aggrieved and fearful. "Ninety-one...ninety-two...I am worried sick about daddy," the son will tell me. "Ninety-nine...hundred...god, he is sweating slightly on the upper lip! Could it be heart attack?!"

I could tell such people that superstition can cause senility in the young, but physiological processes cannot be influenced by social niceties. Sadly, I have to defer to mumbo jumbo because I can no longer challenge people to throw their best *buri-nazar* punch at my father. But I am on surer ground when it comes to kids. I don't have children of my own, but my four-month-old niece is currently my guest and is under my care.

In my pre-niece days, I had to be careful about my spontaneous burst of affection triggered by the sight of a miniature life form wriggling in the aroma of milk, powder, and human purity. Some parents would be so worried about *nazar* that I would be tempted to carry a *nazar suraksha kavach* as gift, merely to be able to say, "How cute!"

As for my niece, she has drawn admiration for her ravishing looks, voice, and complexion — which is as limpid as V S Naipaul's writing, owing to her wise avoidance of junk food and alcohol. Not only do I accept complimentary gurgling on her behalf, but I actively solicit it by posting her pictures on Facebook.

Of course, my abashedly public devotion to the child reflects my pride in her. But it is also meant to assure some people that *nazar* is no more harmful than myopia. In fact, if I ever buy a truck, my bumper slogan would be: *Buri nazar waley, terey muh par chasma.*

My argument, prima facie, is borne out by science and indeed by the scriptures. The Ten Commandments do not mention *buri nazar*, and neither does Adi Sankara's Bhaja Govindam, which I turn to for sane advice on life. Adi Sankara advises against lecherousness though:

naaree sthanabhara naabheedesam
drishtvaa maa gaa mohaavesam
etan maamsavasaadi vikaaram
manasi vichintaya vaaram vaaram

The substance of the *sloka* is, "Don't be deluded by the sight of physical beauty of women, the form is nothing but flesh and fat..."

That kind of *buri nazar* is commonplace on Indian roads and at workplaces. As far as I know, no 'sexual harassment *suraksha kavach*' is sold, even on late-late-night teleshopping channels.

Having said all of this, I must admit that there is one superstition supported by empirical power. I have learnt from my boss on the news desk that the day I look at the likely workflow and determine that I can go home early, the exit time is usually 2:00 am. On such days, corrupt ministers who defied courts and gods for months suddenly transform into beacons of propriety and resign ten minutes before deadline.

Economics of death

Jug Suraiya | 14 April 2011

What price do you put on someone you love? That's the real and unasked question in the debate on passive euthanasia — terminating the lives of the incurably ill who are no longer conscious or capable of acting on their own. I recall a family's terrible dilemma which I found myself involved in some years ago.

One of the sisters in the family was stricken by an irreversible and fatal disease that attacks the auto-immune system and for which there is no known cure. The diagnosis had been made too late to try alternative therapies which might have deferred the inevitable. The patient — to whom I was not related but who was as close to me as if she were my own sister — went into a coma and was taken to a state-of-the-art medical facility in Delhi.

The moment she was admitted into the hospital, the patient, in effect, ceased to be a human individual with human attachments of family and loved ones and became instead the property of a team of medical specialists. No longer conscious of where she was or what was happening to her, she was put into an intensive care unit which no one could enter except those who were treating her. We could see her through a glass pane, attached to mechanical devices which took over from her the business of existence: the breathing of the lungs, the beating of the heart, the circulation of blood, the intake of nutrition. She became a machine, linked to other machines.

Regular as clockwork the attendant team of specialists would look in on the patient. Literally look in. Open the door, look at her from the doorway, make a note on clipboards they were carrying and go away. It was a large team and day by day it seemed to get larger. Who are all these people? I asked a nurse. Doctors, she replied.

What sort of doctors? I asked. Special doctors, said the nurse. They were indeed special doctors, as I discovered. One was a dietitian. Another was a dermatologist. Why did a patient unable to take in any nutrition other than through a drip need a dietitian to visit three times a day? No one knew. Why did the patient need a dermatologist's visit every day? No one knew.

But each time these specialists would look in on her, the visit would be put on the bill. Which, like the team of specialists, was daily growing bigger. It was, after all, a state-of-the-art private hospital. With high overheads, including specialists who occupied expensive offices and had to earn fees in order to pay their rentals.

Twice a day we'd go to see the head doctor. No, there was no change in the patient. No, no change could be expected. No one could bring themselves to ask the question that hung in the silence like a thunderclap: How long do we go on like this, how long can we go on?

The family was reasonably well off. But how long could they afford to keep the patient in the hospital? One month? Two? A year? There were other expenses to meet, a son to be educated, futures to be provided for. But how do you put a cut-off price on a life? Even on the life of a machine kept alive by other machines.

The family couldn't do it. So I volunteered. I told the head doctor there was no more money for the ICU, for the machines. The doctor looked thoughtful. I see, he said. There was no talk of the law, or of ethics. No talk of the sanctity of life. No talk of miracle cures.

Sometime that day, we weren't told when, the machines were switched off. The patient stopped being a patient and became a closed file and a final bill. Which the family paid, racked with remorse, feeling that what they were paying was blood money. Was this sum what a life was worth, no more and no less? To the loss of a loved one was added the burden of guilt.

Parliament can legislate on the ethics of euthanasia. Who's going to legislate on the economics of death, and the cost that conscience has to bear? What is the price of someone you love?

An everlasting love

Vinita Dawra Nangia | 08 May 2011

As boundless as a mother's love is for her child, she gets much more in return. It's a love that has her soar the skies and, sometimes, plumb the depths...

The clincher to decide the top three beauties at the recent Pantaloons Femina Miss India 2011 pageant this year was, "A child learns a lot from his mother; what does a mother learn from her child?"

PFMI World Kanishtha had answered, "Mothers can learn to live their dreams from their children." PFMI Earth Hasleen spoke of how mothers can learn to do things uninhibitedly like children. And PFMI International Ankita Shorey said a mother learns unconditional love from her child.

It is not as if a child teaches the mother anything consciously. Nor does this mean that a mother observes her child and learns new tricks. The point is that the experience of motherhood allows one to tap hitherto undiscovered strengths and weaknesses within oneself. As such, Ankita's response was the most appropriate, because it is not from the child that a mother learns, but from within herself. By observing and understanding her own response to this tiny, helpless being she has created, whose very life is in her hands, a woman learns so much not just about herself but about others and rest of the world as well.

Patience, love, forgiveness and a spirit of sacrifice are the most important emotions motherhood teaches. Most new mothers are surprised at the amount of patience they find for their babies. Plumbing the depths and soaring the heights of love to understand your own capacity for loving is something you learn easier as a mother than in any other relationship. In any other role, love has its limitations but a mother's love is boundless.

Have you observed how new moms cannot stop talking about their 'cute' babies or how crazy they are about their kids? All kids are cute and all mothers bonkers over them, but try telling a new mom that! To her it's almost like nobody ever before, nor anyone after her is likely to have a kid! This behaviour is nothing but the mother expressing aloud her own surprise at the amount of love, patience and spirit of sacrifice she is experiencing within herself!

In a romantic relationship, at play are huge expectations and a fair amount of give and take. You want to extract as much pleasure out of this relationship as you give your partner, if not more. The relationship also comes with an exit clause, the possibility of it waning and fading out. As such, a huge amount of insecurity surrounds it, keeping you on your toes around a valued lover.

On the other hand with a child, a mother gives love and care with no expectations. It is a tale of just giving, expecting nothing in return. There is complete security in this one tie, at least till such a stage that the child grows to be an adult. Its very helplessness and dependence on the mother arouses her acute protective maternal instincts. Any mother will tell you of the feeling of complete love that envelops her when the child she is suckling, looks up at her in absolute adoration and trust. There is no love in the world that can come anywhere near what she feels at that moment, no moment that can come nearer perfection. Maternal love is a primal urge that animals are not immune to either. The way a tigress protects her young is legendary, but the same is true of all species. The male animal may father the child and walk away, later even prove to be a threat to the young ones, but a mother feeds and protects her child with her life if need be. Her brand of love is universally accepted and lauded as the most unselfish and selfless.

It is in moments when her child is in danger that a mother realises the inner reserves of strength she possesses; she is capable of taking on anyone and anything in order to protect her child. A child alone can get a mother to ascend to the peak of happiness or plummet to the nadir of grief; extremes of emotion that would remain largely untapped and unfelt otherwise.

The true power of love is revealed to us when we can love

selflessly and without any signs of ego. And once a mother experiences such an emotion with her child, she has unleashed a deep understanding of love and the role it plays in our lives and the Universe. In fact, in that sense, motherhood is as close a spiritual experience as one could hope to achieve within the framework of daily living. And the entire process of having and caring for a child is as creative and satisfying as anything can get. If a mother achieves nothing else in life, she has still achieved this...motherhood.

On the other hand, the love of a child for the mother may not be as unselfish. Recognising the depth of a mother's love, a child learns fast to use it for his own benefit. But love begets love, and so long as the child realises that the mother's love for him is unconditional, he is bound to respond to the best of his capability and capacity.

As an Irish proverb goes, "A man loves his sweetheart the most, his wife the best, but his mother the longest."

Why did this have to happen to me?

Kingshuk Mukherji | 12 April 2011

How many times have my daughters asked "But baba, why did this have to happen to me?" Whenever they threw this question to me, I got pinned onto the back foot. But with kids, as all parents would know, you can't grope for answers, you can't ponder, neither can you afford to press the search button embedded inside your brain. You've to answer, quickly and confidently.

If memory serves me right, the first time my elder one asked me this was when she came home with a fractured right hand. She was playing basketball and a brute tackle had left her with a hairline fracture on her right hand.

She wasn't bothered that the injured hand hurt. She was hassled because she would have to write an exam a week later. "Baba, my grades will go for a toss. I can't hold a pen properly with my other hand, leave alone write a letter," she sobbed. The corners of her large expressive eyes had turned a shade of red and tears were welling up, panic writ bold in them. "Baba, why did this have to happen to me?"

Hmm, a googly, I told myself and instantly readied a quick repartee. Task one was not to get affected by the panic spasms that had by then gripped the child and make light of what she was saying. The only answer — irrational it may sound — that came to my mind was: Ok, so what? Write with your left hand. Yes, you can do it. I took care not to blurt my line out, keeping the tone even, sounding level headed, disguising my own sense of alarm and without sounding dismissive.

"What?" She shrieked. Instead of calming her down, I had made her jump. "I thought I told you I can't grip a pen with my left hand. You can't expect me to perfect the art of writing with my wrong hand in a week's time. You must be crazy."

Awe, I kicked myself, this one had gone up the wrong street. Nevertheless, we had made a start. The need to talk sense had been reinforced, both in her and me. To panic is irrational. Finding a solution is the logical way to go. Have you ever tried it out? Give it a shot, I soldiered on. Imagine pulling it off. It will be a double sundae. You have worked hard and know your lessons well and now if you get your left hand up and running, it'll be a skill that will probably stay with you for a lifetime. You'll be ambidextrous. Fantastic! Besides, it'll be far more worthwhile trying this out than worrying yourself silly over why the guy upstairs thought this was a great time to break your right hand just ahead of your exams. It's an opportunity, silly.

"Silly! How dare you call me silly! It's a life and death question," she said her decibel levels mounting with each syllable. Do you know of anyone who has ever done this in real life? I sensed an opportunity in that question and immediately seized upon it rattling off names, some real others (strictly between you me and the doorpost) imaginary, of those who were equally adept at using both hands with equal ease. If they can do this, why can't you?

Shriek gave way to whine. "They are geniuses. I am not. I am ordinary." By then, she had come down several notches. I concede I needed a real smart one to parry this. Well kid, I told her, you are just as ordinary as you make yourself out to be. If you want to be smart and want to find a solution, you will. Nothing can stop you. It is all in the mind. Besides, accidents will happen. That doesn't mean life will stop dead. You'll have to surmount the difficulty. That's what life is about. Punditry and hot air, but that set her thinking. It gave her a bone to chew upon and kill the tension.

A couple of days, she tried writing with her left hand and it was rather painstaking and what she produced on paper was an indistinguishable scrawl. But she kept trying. I must give it to her.

At the next visit to her orthopaedic, she told him she was

determined to take the exam and even more bent on doing well. The negativism had evaporated. The doc, a wise old man, came up with a solution. He put her in a flexible cast that allowed her to move her thumb and grip a pen. No doubt, it was painful, but she still managed to write.

She took the exam and did reasonably well. She emerged out of the examination hall and told me she had done well and had hardly felt pain. Her drive to write the test and do well had numbed the pain. The other plus: She realized the pointlessness of asking why this had happened to her.

Do we need a censor board at all?

Alok Tiwari | 29 March 2011

The Information and Broadcasting ministry has finally zeroed in on dancer and writer Leela Samson to head the film censor board. She will succeed actor Sharmila Tagore whose term is ending this month. The surprise choice of Bharatnatyam exponent Samson who, though a brilliant dancer, has no experience or background of movies comes after reports that a string of film industry veterans had declined to accept the post. While most of them politely cited other commitments, clearly they wanted to avoid the controversies that usually go with the job.

This might be a good time to ask if we really need a censor board at all, especially one that functions — directly or indirectly — under the government. It has been some years that the body has been renamed from the almost Soviet-sounding Central Board of Film Censors to more benign Central Board of Film Certification. Yet, its functions have remained almost the same. Despite recent refinement of attitudes, it has largely functioned as a government watchdog over movies. Its façade of autonomy wears thin at every test.

Its brief is not very clear, nor its history encouraging. Over the years, it has faulted some of the finest works of Indian filmmakers just because it found the subject too sensitive or its treatment too provocative. On the other hand, it has okayed crassest works for universal exhibition. In its thinking and approach, it has remained at least a generation behind times. Not just that, clearance from the board does not guarantee any protection to filmmaker. Any individual who finds something wrong with the movie is still able to drag the director and producer to court over it.

Basically, I find the idea of a censor board itself an anathema. It is an insult to Indian democracy to have a handful of government-appointed gatekeepers decide what people should or should not see. Films are one of the several media now available to people. They have every right to be as free as printed word. The argument that just because something is audio-visual it has to be strictly regulated has no rational basis. The censor board has continued as relic from our past where a nanny government took on several jobs it had no business to be in. Time has come to junk it.

Films, like content being hawked through any other medium, have to follow basic laws of the land. The filmmakers and distributors could be sued and would be open to judicial injunctions if they incited violence, defamed someone, or showed something obscene. Why is it that they are subject to pre-censorship when other media like TV, newspapers, and websites are not? There is no evidence to suggest that films affect viewer's psyche and behaviour more than the other media. It makes no sense to make moviemakers go through exhaustive and expensive review and appeals processes before bureaucrats when painters and writers can exhibit and publish what they want.

Moreover, in the age of Internet when rawest videos, most provocative political and religious commentary, and even hardcore pornography are available virtually on every computer and mobile device something like a censor board is an anachronism. Just whom are we protecting and from what? If we trust even our 18-year-olds, regardless of their education, to vote and elect a government, why can't we trust the same people to make a good choice of what movies to watch?

These are not new arguments it is just that now it is more necessary than ever to accept their validity. The fact that no respectable person from film industry is ready to accept what is still a powerful position indicates what people in industry think of the organization. The view among viewers, for whose protection and benefit ostensibly the censor board exists, is likely to be no different.

Of course, I realize it may not be politically acceptable to abolish the censor board overnight and move to a totally liberal regime.

Could we, in the interim, have a body purely for certification of films? It would have powers only to categorize the movies in certain well defined niches (For eg universal, parental guidance, 15+ years, and adult) and not to stop its exhibition or demand cuts in certain scenes. Some restrictions on stuff that is purely pornographic may remain but certainly nothing should be stopped because it makes a controversial or provocative political or social point.

Also, this body ought to be managed and run largely by film industry itself, pretty much like chartered accountants run their own affairs through Institute of Chartered Accountants of India. It should also provide a complaint mechanism should somebody find something particularly objectionable in a movie. It would have power to advise or even censure but not to ban. The filmmakers, like any other citizens, would be legally responsible for what they put out. The viewers, as always, would be free to decide what they would spend money to watch.

Mard ko dard nahi hota

Rupam Singh Gupta | 15 April 2011

Boy oh boy! He is a monster when it comes to show of stunts, but is otherwise a softie which makes him adorable. There's no limit to his daredevilry. My heart does a somersault; every time I see him hop on the TV set placed on a 4-feet tabletop from a 2-feet bed and then dive for the bean bag down on the floor. Like a skilled acrobat, he swiftly tucks his chin in his chest lest he bangs his head on the tiled floor. But, he is not lucky always. One slip and he falls flat. But, is quick to collect himself and sits there with hands folded across his chest, silently. "Did you hurt yourself?" I ask him with my heart in my mouth. "Nope," comes a stoic reply. I know he is hurt badly, but doesn't want to show his pain. Oh man, he's not even four!

Mard ko dard nahi hota, rings an old friend's humorous take on man's innate behaviour of restraining himself from shedding tears when hurt. He bears the pain to the point of being superhuman – no matter "how badly he has been beaten or how cruel the torture has been". But, *chot agar dil pe lagi ho to dard hota hai,* says a journo friend, *aur phir dil hi nahi, aankhen bhi zaar-zaar roti hain.* If a heartbroken man says that he is not wounded, he is not bruised and bleeding, then he is lying, he says, citing the case of his close friend, who broke a dozen hearts before meeting the same fate. Tears roll down his cheeks even today while nursing his wounds.

Salon terms the year 2010 as the year of tears for men. Citing an attorney, it states how male "machoism dominated early 70s. Men were not supposed to publicly display emotions as it was viewed as a sign of weakness. But stoicism gave way over the years to sensitivity as a desirable male trait, and by 2010, there were few fears for tears left among well-known American men".

I have seen my father and brothers weep at the *bidaai* of my two elder sisters. I understand their crying as it was done at a time and in a particular circumstance that allowed them to lower their guard without the fear of ridicule. I am sure that they wouldn't be moved enough by a good movie to let a drop out of their tear ducts. Not even by failure or embarrassment. How often we hear moms admonish their little boys, "Stop crying, be a man!" "An oft-repeated phrase, 'be a man' means to look failure, frailty and fear squarely in the face, and not blink," says a feminist and a writer.

But down the years, men have become less inhibited in demonstrating emotions. In fact, we get to see more of this human side of the male now. What was once considered as unmanly, is now being viewed as a quality to have as an asset. The turnaround was ably captured in the Raymond's 'complete man' ad series in 1990s. It broke the stereotypical image of a macho Indian man portrayed in Hindi films. "Raymond actually robbed the man of his *mardangi*," says a columnist. And, instead emerged a "sensitive, vulnerable, versatile, caring, intellectual and fun" man. The next decade saw this softer side becoming more pronounced. Images of men crying openly began to fill the small screen space. TV actors left behind the likes of Archana, Tulsi and Parvati in the tear terrain. "It's cool to cry as it shows that emotions are same for men and women," says a TV actor. Not only on daily soaps, but also on the reality shows more and more men turned on the waterworks. Filmmaker Shekhar Kapur got so overwhelmed by the performance of a group of physically challenged kids on India's Got Talent that he couldn't control his sobbing. Sanjay Dutt — the icon of macho Bollywood heroes — wept on the Indian Idol 5 show after hearing the soul stirring AR Rahman's Sufi number *Khwaja mere khwaja.*

Remember Qutubuddin Ansari! The face that flashed across the world as the face of the Gujarat riots — eyes welling with tears, face covered with mud and dried blood, and hands folded in a plea for mercy. Or, cricketer Kapil Dev, who broke down on Karan Thapar's show when asked if he had a role in match-fixing! And, can we ever forget our Men in Blue shedding the tears of joy and jubilation after winning the World Cup? Yes, the man has arrived — *mard ko bhi dard hota hai...*

Too much tosh on sale

Pritish Nandy | 18 October 2010

We live in solipsistic, self indulgent times. Even if you don't endorse the desperate need for self promotion, as indeed many of us don't, there is too much of parental and peer pressure to simply ignore it. Look at some of the reality shows on TV and you will know what I mean. Grown ups are making a spectacular fool of themselves in front of millions. So are kids, some of them barely struggling to enter puberty but with no qualms about shaking their booty in front of crowds of hired strangers paid to clap at the end of every performance, however stupid or talentless it may be. There is an even bigger audience of idiots out there so desperate to express their opinion on which talent deserves to be protected or sacked that they will shell out Rs 15 per sms. If the channels are to be believed, more votes are polled during these reality shows than during elections, earning the channels a neat profit marketing pure drivel.

I have nothing against drivel as long as we know and recognise it as such. But the problem is that an entire generation is now growing up on tosh masquerading as genius. Just as an entire generation is growing up on tabloid gossip believing it is news. Perhaps I was lucky I grew up in times when some of the India's finest talent in music, art, theatre, movies, poetry flourished. So I can still make out the difference. But a whole new generation is now out there, with blinkers on. They buy anything that's packaged with hype and sold to them as success. They see it as sizzling talent. If you have never heard the music of RD Burman I'm not surprised you think Sajid Wajid is next to God. If you haven't seen Shombhu Mitra on stage, can I blame you if you think Balika Vadhu is the ultimate in staged entertainment?

That is why we need history, knowledge. They context our experience. That is why classics are revered. If you haven't heard Nusrat Fateh Ali sing, how can I blame you for believing that Himesh is the greatest singer of all time? That's the problem with our times. We are too self obsessed, too busy with ourselves to realise that there's much more to our art, music, culture than what we see happening on TV today. How can a critic who has never watched Manmohan Desai or Hrishikesh Mukherjee movies ever figure where our cinema is coming from? Unless you have heard Kishore Kumar or Mukesh sing, how will you ever know where the roots of our popular music lie? No, I am not trying to sell you nostalgia. I am only trying to expand your imagination by assuring you that there's much more to enjoy if only you were to enlarge your scope of sampling beyond Munni's charming exertions.

If you haven't seen Sunil Janah's photographs of the great Bengal famine, how can you ever understand the power and passion of visual journalism? Pablo Bartholomew's one iconic picture of the aftermath of the Bhopal gas leak has survived millions of words to remain the strongest reminder of that human tragedy that still aches our conscience. I see so much abstract art around but nothing compares with the work of my friend Gaitonde who died a lonely, broken man in a Delhi *barsaati*, years after he stopped painting because he thought he had nothing left to say. His works still come up in auctions and sell for a million dollars whereas he died penniless and I know few people today who are even aware of his work. There's no access to it either, apart from a few private collections which remain in godowns collecting dust and appreciating in value to be eventually sold off.

Yes, we have reduced art to auctions, music to reality shows, journalism to staged hysterics on TV, dance to item numbers, religion to unbearably noisy public festivals and the intemperate politics of hate. We have reduced our living literature to boring text books that have to be mugged before exams where your memory and cheating skills are tested more than your knowledge. We have reduced love to V Day cards and bouquets of cut flowers. We have reduced our pride and honour to the crude symbolism of murdering our own kids who want to make a marital choice different from ours. We have reduced all enterprise to the making of profit and bred a nation of carpetbaggers. Raj Kapoor teetered on the edge of bankruptcy all his life even as he made his most memorable films. Guru Dutt killed himself because he felt unfulfilled. Today's film makers only boast their box office takes.

Are we losing out something somewhere or is this a new culture we want to build where the past does not exist and the future can go to hell?

Chul Bull Pandey!

Anshul Chaturvedi | 11 September 2010

Hell, what a movie.

The promos have had everybody hooked — the fab songs, peppy, rocking, easy on the lips. Ok, all that, and, aahh... Munnie! And the movie — going by the way the first day bookings were going, I assume half the country would have seen it by now — is, in essence, what we loved and saw on TV all these weeks: the completely engaging tamasha songs, Munnie, the thoroughly outrageously exaggerated swagger of the one and only Salman Khan, Munnie, the scintillating one-liners, Munnie...ok, ok, I concede, she only comes once in the movie. Big deal! All of this, the dance, the drama, the action, looked so much bigger, louder, how do you put it, err, so much more Dabangg on the big screen, just the way one thought they would. Solid impact hai, bhai!

Oh, yes, at intervals amidst these impactful elements, there were also some scenes and some dialogues and some well hidden reasons why Arbaaz and Vinod Khanna and Dimple and a few other people seemed to be part of what could be very forgivingly be called a story. And there's Sonu, good shirtless competition to our hero. Many have praised the debutante Sonakshi, but — not that I am a cine critic — her USP eluded me. The movie, of course, will rock — but, umm, Kaho Na Pyar Hai rocking didn't do much for Amisha, did it?

To repeat, there's Salman, and the rest, and the only thing missing is a script. In a day and age when director after director has told me in interview after interview that films flop and people don't watch movies because we don't have good scripts, you have a blockbuster-in-the-making that HAS no script . But, hell, whoever asked anyone to watch this to decipher the script's sophistication. You want to do that, go watch Inception, dude.

So, realistic cinema be damned, we rediscover that the Indian audience loves the SUPERSTAR. Yes, we know he's doing stuff that can't be done, we know it's bizarre, but we love it. And why just paint it as an escapist Indian mindset — we know Asterix's magic potion doesn't really exist but we loved it when he socks the Romans, we know there's no Krypton but we loved Superman's escapades — so what's different here, haan? That in-your-face style power — *ishtyle, tashan*, presence, call it what you will — not everyone can pull it off. Sallu so bloody well can. Even when he's hamming, he does it so audaciously, you want to clap by the time you're over the shock. Make no mistake, and keep that snooty remark to yourself — we're all front benchers here!

Suniel Shetty was saying nostalgically, in a chat with me a few days back when he was in Delhi, that while today's movies are more evolved, perhaps, he misses the 'superstars' on screen, the sort of stuff that made him stand up on his seat and whistle and applaud when he was a kid, the sort of dum of a star that would have people throwing coins on screen when the hero said something that everyone by then knew by heart — rationality be damned.

Well, Salman just gave you back that raw star on screen, Suneil. Go, whistle!

About the Bloggers

Bachi Karkaria

Bachi Karkaria's Erratica and its cheeky sign-off character, Alec Smart, have had a growing league of followers since 1994 when the column began in the Metropolis on Saturday. It now appears on the Edit Page of the Times of India, every Friday. It takes a sly dig at whatever has inflated political/celebrity egos, and got public knickers in a twist that week.

SA Aiyar

Swaminathan S Anklesaria Aiyar is consulting editor of The Economic Times. A popular columnist and TV commentator, Swami has been called "India's leading economic journalist" by Stephen Cohen of the Brookings Institution. "Swaminomics" has been appearing as a weekly column in The Times of India since 1990.

Jug Suraiya

An associate editor with the Times of India, Jug Suraiya writes two regular columns for the print edition, Jugular Vein, which appears every Friday, and Second Opinion, which appears on Wednesdays. His blog takes a contrarian view of topical and timeless issues, political, social, economic and speculative.

Shobhaa De

One of India's most popular writers, Shobhaa De has seen it all: life as a model, a copywriter, a journalist, a socialite, a scriptwriter, a bestselling novelist and a busy mother of six children. "Politically Incorrect", appearing as a column in The Times of India, carries her sharp observations on politics, society, economy and relationships.

Pritish Nandy

Pritish Nandy writes, paints, makes movies and occasionally, when he wins an election, sits in Parliament. He has been writing for The Times of India for over 26 years. In "Extraordinary Issue", he talks to all those who find his views controversial, challenging, charming or even utterly despicable.

Swapan Dasgupta

Well-known journalist and political commentator Swapan Dasgupta has worked for many leading Indian publications, including The Times of India. He thinks the Right is an endangered community in India's English-language media. "Right & Wrong" is one of the few voices of the community.

Ranjan Roy

Ranjan Roy is editor of Times News Network. He has been a news agency reporter in various parts of the world and has covered politics and wars in South Asia, Southeast Asia and Afghanistan. He has covered the United Nations while based in New York from where he relocated to India.

TK Arun

TK Arun is the Editor of Opinion in The Economic Times. In his blog Cursor, TK writes on various issues ranging from economy to politics to national issues.

Gurcharan Das

Bestselling author Gurcharan Das is a former CEO of Procter & Gamble India. He was VP & MD, P&G Worldwide, when he took early retirement in 1995 to become a full-time writer. Das graduated with honors from Harvard University in Philosophy and Politics.

Kingshuk Nag

Kingshuk Nag, Resident Editor of The Times of India, Hyderabad, considers himself a jack of all trades. Accordingly, his blog, Masala Noodles, is about life, people, politics, economics, history and what have you. He promises the blog will have a lot of spice and "round and round" noodles, as in the twists and turns of our daily existence.

Vinita Dawra Nangia

Vinita Dawra Nangia is a Senior Editor with The Times of India. The blog O-zone reflects her incisive insights into the world around, offering a newer way of looking at life, people and the situations they find themselves in. The blog puts forth practical, feel-good ways of dealing with contemporary chaos, leading to a guilt-free life!

Anshul Chaturvedi

Anshul Chaturvedi attempts to scrutinise high society and the glam world from the vantage point that his current job as the Delhi Times editor gives him. Being a 'philosopher' isn't his cup of tea, but he pleads guilty to philosophising on random issues - sometimes. As will his blog!

Abheek Barman

Abheek Barman is Consulting Editor, ET Now. He is one of India's most influential financial journalists and commentators. Barman writes a widely read column, Folk Theorem, for The Economic Times.

Bobilli Vijay Kumar

Bobilli Vijay Kumar is TOI's National Sports Editor. He writes a weekly column, mainly on cricket; he has many interests, though, going way beyond sport itself: you can't keep him out of a movie hall or away from Floyd or Doors.

Shobhan Saxena

Shobhan Saxena is an editor with Sunday Times of India. Though his interests range from international issues, human rights and politics to art & culture, what really fascinates him is the extraordinary lives of ordinary people -- the men and women on the street, their lives and their views on everything under the sun.

Rajesh Kalra

Rajesh Kalra is the Chief Editor of Times Internet and responsible for innovations. He is an avid sportsman, a trained high-altitude mountaineer and a marathoner. His blog, Random Access, will cover issues that take into account these varied interests.

Raja Bose

Raja Bose, resident editor of The Times of India in Chandigarh, has travelled from the land of the Red, Communist, Bengal to the land of Green Revolution, Punjab, with stopovers in Modi's Gujarat and Lalu's Bihar, spending 17 years with his ears to the ground,going on, truly, a journey without maps.

Indrani Bagchi

Indrani Bagchi is The Times of India's diplomatic editor. She calls this blog a wide canvas through which she looks at the world and how India responds to it.

CP Surendran

CP Surendran is a senior editor at The Times of India, Delhi. Surendran is also the author of four volumes of poetry: Gemini II (Penguin Viking), Posthumous Poems (Penguin), Canaries on the Moon (Yeti) and Portraits of the Space We Occupy (Harper Collins). His poems have been widely anthologized in India and abroad.

Robin David

Robin David is senior assistant editor of The Times of India, Ahmedabad. He has written on a range of subjects from education to environment to communal violence and politics. A big fan of fast bowling, he loves bowling bouncers and fending them off.

Alok Tiwari

Alok Tiwari is deputy resident editor of The Times of India, Nagpur. In a career of nearly 30 years, he has reported on practically every beat. He is deeply interested in social and environmental issues and loves to travel, especially in wildlife rich forests of central India.

Nauzer K Bharucha

Nauzer K Bharucha is a senior assistant editor at The Times of India, Mumbai. He has been a hardcore reporter with a ringside view of the functioning of the government and its various agencies. He has exposed a number of scams mainly involving public land and award of multi-crore civic projects.

Kannan Somasundaram

Kannan Somasundaram is an assistant editor at the Times of India, Ahmedabad. He began his career in journalism as a film and book reviewer. The amorality and violence of modern cinema and literature prepared him well for subsequent stints with news desks dealing with Indian politics.

Nandita Sengupta

Nandita Sengupta works as a senior assistant editor with The Times of India, Delhi. Her blog is mainly about women and the young and about men when they deserve a mention.

Sudeshna Sen

Sudeshna Sen is foreign editor of The Economic Times, working out of London for the past three years.

Kingshuk Mukherji

Kingshuk Mukherji is first a parent who loves listening to and understanding all children have to say on everything — from their friends, to school, their peers and their teachers. He is also an associate editor with The Times of India.

Rupam Singh Gupta

Rupam Singh Gupta is a deputy news editor at The Times of India, Ahmedabad. A postgraduate in English literature, her areas of interest include education, craft and gender.

Saibal Bose

The blogger is currently the sports editor of The Times of India's Jaipur edition. He has been covering sporting events for around 15 years now.